22.95 ✓

PERFORMANCE APPRAISALS

THE SUNDAY TIMES BUSINESS SKILLS SERIES

"excellent ... well worth reading"

Christopher Lorenz, the *Financial Times*

The Sunday Times Business Skills Series is an up-to-the-minute collection of books covering essential management topics in the three key areas of total quality management, personal skills and leadership skills.

Combining current management theory and practice with detailed case examples and practical advice, each book provides a definitive stand-alone summary of best management practice in a specific field. While each book is complete in itself, books in the series have been carefully co-ordinated to complement *The Sunday Times* Business Skills video training package of the same name produced by Taylor Made Films (see inside back flap for more details).

Books already published in the series:

PERFORMANCE APPRAISALS
Martin Fisher
ISBN 0 7494 1441 3

MANAGING CHANGE
Philip Sadler
ISBN 0 7494 1343 3

EFFECTIVE NEGOTIATING
Colin Robinson
ISBN 0 7494 1344 1

BUILDING YOUR TEAM
Rupert Eales-White
ISBN 0 7494 1342 5

ACHIEVING BS EN ISO 9000
Peter Jackson and David Ashton
ISBN 0 7494 1440 5

PERFORMANCE APPRAISALS

Martin Fisher

KOGAN
PAGE

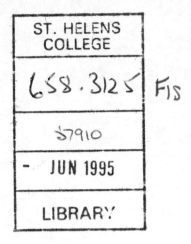
First published in 1995

Apart from any fair dealing for the purposes of research or private study, or
criticism or review, as permitted under the Copyright, Designs and Patents Act,
1988, this publication may only be reproduced, stored or transmitted, in any form
or by any means, with the prior permission in writing of the publishers, or in the
case of reprographic reproduction in accordance with the terms of licences issued
by the Copyright Licensing Agency. Enquiries concerning reproduction outside
those terms should be sent to the publishers at the undermentioned address:

Kogan Page Limited
120 Pentonville Road
London N1 9JN

© Martin Fisher, 1995

British Library Cataloguing in Publication Data

A CIP record for this book is available from the British Library.

ISBN 0 7494 1441 3

Typeset by Saxon Graphics Ltd, Derby.
Printed in England by Clays Ltd, St Ives plc

Contents

Introduction

This book is complementary to the Sunday Times video training package on *Leadership: Performance Appraisals* in their Business Skills series. Its aim is to help the reader understand:

○ The purpose, benefits and process of performance appraisal (Part 1).
○ The foundations of performance appraisal defining jobs, objectives and competences (Part 2).
○ How to conduct an appraisal discussion (Part 3).
○ How to follow up an appraisal discussion with continuing informal reviews, using coaching and counselling skills as required (Part 4).
○ How to introduce a performance appraisal scheme (Part 5).

Throughout the book the following terms are used:

○ **Appraiser** to mean the person organising and conducting the performance appraisal through formal and informal discussions and reviews.
○ **Appraisee** to mean the person whose performance is being appraised.

Part 1

THE ESSENCE OF PERFORMANCE APPRAISAL

1

Purpose of Performance Appraisal

The purpose of performance appraisal is to improve the organisation's performance through the enhanced performance of individuals.

OBJECTIVES OF PERFORMANCE APPRAISAL

When people think about performance appraisal they often refer to a number of more specific positive objectives such as:

○ to review past performance;
○ to assess training needs;
○ to help develop individuals;
○ to audit the skills within an organisation;
○ to set targets for future performance;
○ to identify potential for promotion.

More negatively they may believe that performance appraisal is simply used by the organisation to apportion blame and to provide a basis for disciplinary action. Some people see it as a stick that management has introduced with which to beat people. And if this is their attitude – with or without cause – performance appraisal is doomed to failure.

Even if the more positive objectives are built into the scheme, problems may arise because:

○ they may not all be achievable;

○ they can cause conflict.

For example, an appraisee is less likely to be open about any shortcomings in past performance during a process that affects pay or promotion prospects, or which might be perceived as leading to disciplinary action.

It is therefore important that performance appraisal should have specific objectives. Not only should the objectives be clear but they should form part of the organisation's whole strategy. In this way the key objectives can be incorporated into the appraisals, highlighting areas for improvement, new directions and opportunities.

A good definition of the objective of performance appraisal was given by Alan Fowler in *PM Plus*, June 1991. He suggested that:

> Staff work best when they know what they have to do, how well they have to do it, and how well they are thought to have done, so they need to talk to their managers at least once a year about this, and their managers need to take their staff's views into account when setting work goals and deciding who needs what training.

The following are some examples of the definitions used by various organisations:

Cambridgeshire County Council, for example, is quite clear that the objectives of performance review meetings are to:

○ look back on what has been accomplished;

○ look forward to what needs to be accomplished;

○ identify how individuals can be helped to improve their contribution in their present jobs;

○ clarify the job holder's career prospects, aspirations and intentions.

Note that these objectives are all positive. There is no reference to 'identifying weaknesses'; no implication that the process is about 'attaching blame'.

The National Australia Group Ltd states that their scheme is:

...based on the simple idea that when people know and understand what is expected of them, and have been able to take part in forming these expectations, they can and will perform to meet them.

The Group gave the following reasons for introducing the scheme:

O We need to be offered encouragement and support to perform well.

O When our performance is assessed it needs to be as objective as possible.

O We should all be part of the same process of performance assessment.

O We need to believe and have confidence that the system is fair to everyone.

O We need everybody to be trained so that the approach is fully understood and can be applied consistently.

O We all need to be involved in the process with advance information, time for preparation and an opportunity to assess ourselves.

At MENCAP the aims and principles of their performance management and development system were defined as follows:

Aims

O To increase mutual understanding of performance requirements.

O To note and recognise achievements.

O To note and analyse any problems in meeting requirements.

O To provide the opportunity to discuss aspirations and concerns about career prospects and the present job.

O To define or redefine future objectives.

O To agree action plans.

O To agree self-development and training needs.

Principles

O Concentrates on developing strengths as well as addressing performance problems.

○ Based on open and constructive discussion.

○ An everyday and natural management process, not just a once-a-year event and not just a form-filling exercise.

BP Exploration defined the objectives of their performance management system as follows:

> Our stated objective is to achieve a 'best in class' world position. We are dependent on the contribution of each and every one of our people to get there. We need to focus on performance – how to do everything we do better – and this means how we manage our people just as much as it means discovering new oilfields, improving our profitability, managing our costs, or upgrading our public image.
>
> We need to focus on how, on a day by day basis, we deliver performance improvements – even if what we are already doing is of a very high standard. To achieve this we need to change the way we work together and the way performance is discussed. Managers and others responsible for reviewing performance will be assessed on how well they do this.

HP Information plc have defined the objectives of their performance appraisal systems as follows:

○ To improve performance management in HP Information plc.

○ To review past and present work performance.

○ To improve future performance.

○ To set performance objectives.

○ To identify training and development needs.

○ To provide a rational basis for salary recommendations.

○ To develop communications and working relationships.

Note that one of the objectives of this scheme is to provide data for pay proposals. Although, as noted above, this can cause problems, many organisations do include a rating system in their schemes which influences performance-related pay awards. Their reason for doing this is quite clear: if you are going to reward people according to their performance, your decision must be based on a proper review and assessment of their performance.

This is in accordance with one of the basic principles of any pay-for-performance system: that the reward should be clearly and fairly related to the contribution. But this still raises the problem of a conflict between the 'developmental' aspects of the scheme (ie looking forward to how improved performance can be achieved) and the financial reward aspects. Many people argue convincingly that if these two aspects are mixed up in one review process both parties will focus their attention on the financial outcomes and neglect what may be the much more important developmental aspects. One of the fundamental aims of the performance review process, they say, is to motivate people, and trying to do this by offering pay as the main means of motivation detracts from the impact of the other powerful motivators – recognition, praise and the opportunity to succeed.

Realistically, however, if it is believed that performance-related pay is an important means of motivation, it must be based on some form of rating. To get over this difficulty, some organisations avoid rating altogether at the time of the performance review and provide for that meeting to focus on performance and development issues rather than pay. A separate rating will then be made at a later date for performance pay purposes. There will, of course, be a 'read-across' from that rating to the outcome of the formal appraisal discussion and any subsequent informal discussions. After all, performance pay is supposed to be related to performance. But this approach requires the pay part to be kept quite distinct.

BENEFITS

The benefits of a successful appraisal scheme can be summed up as follows:

For the organisation

1. Improved performance throughout the organisation due to:
   — more effective communication of the organisation's objectives and values;

— increased sense of cohesiveness and loyalty;

— improved relationships between managers and staff;

— managers who are better equipped to use their leadership skills and to motivate and develop their staff.

2. Improved overview of the tasks performed by each member of staff.

3. Identification of ideas for improvement.

4. Expectations and long-term views can be developed.

5. Training and development needs identified more clearly.

6. A culture of continuous improvement and success can be created and maintained.

7. People with potential can be identified and career development plans formulated to cater for future staff requirements.

8. The message is conveyed that people are valued.

For the appraiser

1. The opportunity to develop an overview of individual jobs and complete departments.

2. Identification of ideas for improvements.

3. Increased job satisfaction.

4. Increased sense of personal value.

5. The opportunity to link team and individual objectives and targets with departmental and organisational objectives.

6. The opportunity to clarify expectations of the contribution the manager expects from teams and individuals.

7. The opportunity to re-prioritise targets.

8. A means of forming a more productive relationship with staff based on mutual trust and understanding.

For the appraisee

1. Increased motivation.

2. Increased job satisfaction.

3. Increased sense of personal value.

4. A clear understanding of what is expected and what needs to be done to meet expectations.

5. The opportunity to discuss work problems and how they can be overcome.

6. The opportunity to discuss aspirations and any guidance, support or training needed to fulfil these aspirations.

7. Improved working relationships with the manager.

The means by which these objectives and benefits are achieved are summarised in the next chapter.

2

The Approach to Performance Appraisal: Process and Content

PROCESS

Performance appraisal is a process of management. It is not a 'scheme' devised by the personnel department for managers to use in accordance with the directives of that department, and generating completed forms which are stowed away in employees' dossiers and then forgotten.

Performance Appraisal as a Natural Process of Management

Performance appraisal is a natural process of management for three reasons:

Measuring performance – performance appraisal can be used as a means of measuring performance in accordance with the adage: 'if you can't measure it you can't manage it'. But the purpose of measurement is to indicate not only where things are not going according to plan (ie there is a negative variance from the antici-pated result) but also to identify where things are going well (a positive variance) so that steps can be taken to build on success. Performance appraisal is a means for creating and maintaining a 'climate of success in the organization'. The chief executive of a large and successful health care trust was recently asked about his philosophy of management. Among other things, he said: 'We have a success-oriented strategy in which we expect people to succeed and if they don't, we help them to succeed.'

Improving performance – building a climate of success involves taking specific steps to improve the performance of individuals or teams. Because managers depend on that performance, they have a major and continuing responsibility to take whatever action is necessary to improve it. This is an entirely natural process of management and whenever anyone completes a task or project good managers will consciously or unconsciously ask themselves:

O How well was that done?

O Could it have been done better?

O Did I pick the right person?

O Did I brief that person properly?

O In what ways, if any, does this person need to improve?

O What guidance or help can I provide this person to ensure that better results are achieved next time?

We may focus on specific events or incidents but, cumulatively, these build up to an overriding impression of the individual's ability. This could be summed up in the same way as Prime Minister Attlee did to a cabinet minister whom he had just sacked and who asked him why he had taken this drastic action: 'Not up to the job' was the laconic answer. Normally it is necessary to be much more specific than that. A detailed picture is usually built up over time of strengths and areas for improvement as a basis for taking action. But this picture may be impressionistic and performance appraisal aims to provide for more systematic and thought-through conclusions by reference to specific facts and behaviours which have produced identifiable results.

Exercising leadership – there are many ways of defining leadership. Basically, however, it is about getting things done through people. Leaders point the way and ensure that everyone gets there. Leadership is about encouraging and inspiring individuals and teams to give their best to achieve a desired result. Managers as leaders have to achieve the task. That is why they and their teams exist. The leader's role is to ensure that the team's purpose is fulfilled. If it is not, the result is frustration, disharmony, criticisms and, eventually perhaps, disintegration of the group.

Achieving the task involves leaders in getting answers to the following questions:

○ What needs to be done and why?

○ What results have to be achieved?

○ What problems have to be overcome?

○ Is the solution to these problems straightforward or is there a measure of ambiguity?

○ Is this a crisis situation?

○ What is the time-scale for completing the task?

In the light of this analysis leaders have to take whatever steps are necessary to motivate the individuals in their team and also, importantly, to develop good teamwork. Motivating individuals is a matter of:

○ Understanding their needs – are they interested primarily in money, security, status, advancement, achievement or what?

○ Remembering that money is not the only reward that most people need and want. People can also be motivated by recognition, praise and the opportunity to make the best use of their skills and abilities and, indeed, to enhance them.

○ Bearing in mind the importance of expectations as an influence on motivation. A reward, whether financial or non-financial, will be much more effective when people know what they can get if they work well enough.

○ Creating conditions where individuals can best satisfy their own needs by directing their efforts towards achieving the success of their team, department and, ultimately, the organisation. This is why one of the arts of leadership is to get people to think for themselves about what they can and should do and by getting them to understand and agree to the standards and targets they are expected to achieve.

O Recognising the fact that people can be motivated by the work itself if it satisfies their need for responsibility and achievement. This can be done by:

— increasing individual responsibility, 'empowering' them;

— giving them more scope to vary the methods, sequence and pace of work;

— giving people a complete natural unit of work, thus reducing specialisation;

— giving people the control information to monitor their own performance.

The process of performance appraisals, as will be explained later in this chapter and in the rest of this book, is essentially a means for managers to develop and improve their leadership skills in each of the areas described above.

The Essential Elements of the Process

The essential feature of performance appraisal is that it provides a flexible means for managers, and those whom they manage, to operate as partners but within a framework that describes how they can best work together.

Performance appraisal is a process for establishing shared understanding about what is to be achieved, and an approach to managing and developing people in a way which increases the probability that it will be achieved in the short and long term. It is not therefore just a system driven by managements to manage the performance of their employees. It is also an approach to managing and developing people which enables them to manage their own performance and development within the framework of clear objectives and standards which have been agreed jointly with their managers. It does not absolve managers from the responsibility to develop their staff through counselling, coaching and training. However, it does place people in a situation where they can be more in control of the consequences of their own actions.

The concepts of 'empowerment' and continuous development or improvement are important words that have entered into the performance appraisal vocabulary in recent years. In Charles Handy's words (*The Age of Unreason*, Business Books, 1991) performance management or appraisal can help managers to:

O be teachers, counsellors and friends, as much or more than they are commanders and judges;

O trust people to use their own methods to achieve the manager's own ends;

O delegate on the basis of a positive will to trust and to enable, and a willingness to be trusted and enabled;

O become 'post-heroic' leaders who know that every problem can be solved in such a way as to develop people's capacity to handle it.

All these points made by Charles Handy are important but the last one is particularly relevant to the process of performance appraisal where leadership skills are deployed to help people to help themselves.

One important aspect of the process should be emphasised. This is, that performance appraisal should be owned and driven by line managers. It is not a system which is run by the personnel department.

Skills Required

The skills required by managers to carry out a performance appraisal process are often underestimated. They need to know how to agree clear, measurable and achievable objectives with their staff. They need to know how to define and assess competence requirements. They have to provide helpful feedback and know, not only how to commend staff on their achievements in appraisal discussion meetings (which is not too difficult), but also how to coach them and help them to recognise where their performance has been substandard and needs to be improved (which can be much harder).

Properly carried out, performance appraisal implies a marked shift in the relationship between managers and their staff. The manager is faced with a new and more challenging situation: feedback, coaching and counselling skills and the ability to handle and encourage upward appraisal all come to the fore.

However, performance appraisal does not require managers to act out of character. In fact this would be most undesirable. It is no use managers being sweetly reasonable and consultative during the appraisal discussion and then reverting to their autocratic, directive type of behaviour for the rest of the year. This sort of behaviour would only confirm the suspicions of some people that appraisal is a meaningless affair. What such managers can be persuaded to do, however, is to learn that the skills of performance appraisal, as described later in this book, can help them to get better results from their staff and that some modification of their behaviour during the course of their day-to-day work would have beneficial results in the shape of improved performance.

CONTENT

The content of performance appraisal needs to be examined under four headings:

1. *What* is to be appraised – the factors to be taken into account by appraisers and appraisees.
2. *How* appraisals will take place – the methods to be used.
3. *When* formal appraisals will be carried out – at yearly, half-yearly or even quarterly.
4. *What* needs to be done to ensure the appraisal is a continuing process and, as part of this process, to use counselling and coaching skills to improve skills and performance.

What Should Be Appraised?

At one stage in their development, merit rating, performance review, performance assessment or performance appraisal schemes (these terms were used more or less interchangeably) relied mainly on the assessment of personality characteristics. Appraisers often were asked to rate appraisees, using scales of one to five or whatever, on such characteristics as tact, willingness, enthusiasm and maturity.

This approach was for subordinates in effect to be examined by their superiors on the extent to which they exhibited the 'right' characteristics. Managers were being put in the position of psychologists and required to make subjective ratings without any point of reference except their own opinions. Personality traits became an issue and, in effect, managers were being asked to play a god-like role, passing judgements. It is no wonder that many managers refused to play this game, however vigorously they were urged to do so by the personnel department. And if, in response to *force majeure*, they did conduct reviews, they tended to be perfunctory affairs which avoided the real issues and resulted in a bland and meaningless assessment or a set of ticks in boxes which were equally meaningless.

The management by objectives movement which flourished in the 1960s and 1970s was an attempt to overcome this problem by concentrating on results. Inputs in the form of the behaviour of individuals in achieving or not achieving results were not really considered. This approach removed the personality issue from the agenda and concentrated on measurable outputs. From the point of view of objectivity this was a major improvement, but management by objectives as a technique fell into disrepute because it was propped up by reams of paperwork and because it concentrated so much on outputs that it neglected to analyse the reasons for the results achieved in terms of the actual behaviour of individuals – what they actually did or did not do and how they did it. Consequently, management by objectives often failed to provide a satisfactory basis for considering how performance could be improved by reference to those behaviours.

More recent thinking has resulted in an approach which says, in effect, that there are four things you need to look at when you are appraising performance:

1. **Inputs** what the job holders bring to the job in the shape of their knowledge and skills (sometimes referred to as their 'attributes' which are defined as what people need to know and be able to do to perform their job effectively.

2. **Process** the behaviours of job holders in applying their knowledge and skills to the delivery of results. These are sometimes referred to as competences. These describe the behaviour required of people to carry out their job effectively. Such behavioural characteristics can differentiate between highly effective and less effective performers in a given role under such headings as personal drive, analytical power, team management and leadership and ability to communicate.

3. **Outputs** the measurable or at least observable results of the behaviour exhibited by job holders.

4. **Outcomes** the ultimate impact of the job holders on the results of their teams or departments and their overall contribution to achieving the objectives of the organization.

In practice the new approach to performance appraisals concentrates on two aspects:

1. What the individual brings to the job in terms of attributes and behaviour (summarised under the heading of 'input').

2. What results are achieved in terms of outputs and outcomes (referred to as 'outputs').

These concepts of input and output as the basis of appraisal are based on an understanding of the content of the job – what the job holder does as expressed in a job description or role definition. The preparation of job descriptions is covered in Chapter 3. Expectations are expressed as objectives, targets, standards of performance or competence requirements, and how these are defined is considered in Chapter 4.

How Should Appraisal Take Place?

The foundation of performance appraisal is provided by what the job holder is expected to do as defined in a job description and by reference to agreed objectives. The performance appraisal process built on this foundation can be described as a cycle (as shown in Figure 2.1) consisting of:

○ preparation for the appraisal discussion;
○ the formal appraisal discussion;
○ informal reviews.

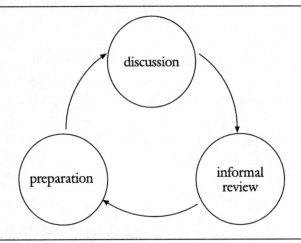

Figure 2.1   The performance appraisal cycle

The preparation section of the cycle covers the pre-meeting work of the appraiser and the appraisee who both review results in the light of previously agreed objectives and decide on any matters they want to raise at the appraisal discussion.

The formal appraisal section of the cycle is concerned with:

○ conducting the appraisal discussion;
○ overcoming any problems emerging during the appraisal;
○ concluding the appraisal by recording the results, agreeing action plans and, as necessary, obtaining another view from the appraiser's manager (the 'grandparent'), to ensure that a fair and thorough appraisal has taken place.

The informal review section of the cycle consists of:

O informal discussions which take place as and when required and may involve updating objectives or performance plans;

O the processes of coaching and counselling, which help to implement the developmental and performance improvement programmes.

When Appraisals Should Take Place

Formal appraisal discussions are often held annually but some fast moving organisations prefer to have them twice a year or even more frequently, say at quarterly intervals. When employees are working on projects, as in a consultancy firm, there may be an appraisal after each assignment but there would still be an overall review at the end of the year. Some organisations hold 'milestone' meetings at appropriate times to review progress towards achieving objectives, work plans or projects. Others hold meetings two or three times a year, the main purpose of which is to review and update objectives. Many organisations require an annual or twice yearly meeting but leave it to the appraiser to decide if any additional meetings are necessary.

Ensuring That Appraisal is a Continuing Process

To ensure that appraisal is not just seen as a once-a-year event to be got over as quickly as possible it is necessary to emphasise the continuing nature of the process in briefing and training. Appraisers and appraisees should understand that feedback and appraisal are in effect everyday occurrences.

PERFORMANCE APPRAISAL AND PERFORMANCE MANAGEMENT

The terms appraisal and performance management are sometimes used interchangeably, but there is a difference between them. Performance management systems will always include performance appraisal or review schemes as a central part of the process, but performance appraisal schemes can operate which do not exhibit the full characteristics of a performance management system which in its most developed form:

○ is concerned with the total performance of the organisation and how the results achieved by individuals and teams contribute to that performance;

○ is seen as much more of an integrating process – integrating corporate, functional, team and individual objectives and linked more closely with other aspects of human resource management;

○ is treated as a normal process of management, not an administrative chore imposed by the personnel department;

○ concerns all members of the organisation as partners in the process – it is not something handed down by bosses to subordinates;

○ is concerned as much with team performance as individual performance;

○ is a continuous process, not relying on a once-a-year formal review – in the words of Alan Fowler ('Performance Management: The MBO of the 90s?', *Personnel Management*, July, 1990): 'In today's fast-moving world, any idea that effective performance management can be tied neatly to a single annual date is patently absurd';

○ can provide a basis for performance-related pay decisions where such schemes exist, but much more care is taken over the development of rating systems and achieving consistency in ratings;

○ may not include ratings at all if the process is used primarily for developmental and performance improvement purposes;

○ does not rely on elaborate forms or procedures – the records of agreements and reviews may be retained by managers and individuals and are sometimes not held by the personnel department;

○ recognises the need for thorough training in the skills required to agree objectives, provide feedback, review performance and coach and counsel employees;

○ overall, attaches much more importance to the 'processes' of forming agreements, managing performance throughout the year and monitoring and reviewing results than to the content of what is often referred to as a 'performance management system' – by implication, a set of mechanisms to get people to do certain things in certain ways.

At Boots the Chemist the features of their performance management system are:

○ The company goals and the store, department and individual goals are all linked.

○ The process focuses on the performance of the organisation as a whole.

○ Individuals know what is expected of them.

○ It links performance objectives, review, reward and individual development.

○ It is owned by line managers.

The approaches to performance appraisal described in the rest of the book do, however, have most of these characteristics. The name may be different but the process is essentially the same.

Part 2

THE FOUNDATION OF PERFORMANCE APPRAISAL

3

Defining Job Content

Performance appraisal assesses how well people have been doing and what they must do to be even better in the future. This is carried out by reference to the content of the job they do and what they are expected to achieve in each aspect of their work. The starting point when preparing for appraisal is therefore job content – the overall purpose of the job and the main tasks or duties (often called principal accountabilities or key result areas) involved in carrying out the job. Each of these main tasks involve achieving certain objectives which may be defined as quantified targets, standards of performance or specific tasks or projects to be completed. To carry them out effectively, job holders require certain levels of knowledge and skills and have to display competence in carrying out their tasks.

The first preparatory step in the performance appraisal process is therefore the agreement of job content between the appraiser and the appraisee. This will be expressed in the form of a job description or role definition. These terms are sometimes used interchangeably but job descriptions often concentrate more on a straight definition of the tasks the job holder has to accomplish, while role definitions will also refer in greater depth to the part or role the job holder is expected to play in contributing to team, departmental or organisational results. This chapter concentrates on how such job or role descriptions are prepared while the next chapter considers methods of setting and agreeing the various types of objectives and analysing skills and competences.

It is, however, necessary to emphasise at this stage that in defining the content of a job, the aim should be to ensure that the definition of each main task indicates broadly the aim of the task, thus providing the basis for a definition of objectives. In practice, what happens in most jobs is that there are a number of standing or continuing objectives which may not need to be revised very often. The basis of such standing objectives can be spelled out in the job description, although this may need to be amplified with a definition of the standard of performance required on a continuing basis, quantified wherever possible. For example, a customer service assistant who has to reply to complaints may have a permanent standard to achieve of replying to or at least acknowledging a query within 24 working hours and, if an immediate answer is not possible, obtaining it and letting the customer know within three working days. This standard may not alter from year to year, although at some stage it may be decided that customer service levels must be increased and that complete answers must be supplied within, say, two working days.

THE FRAMEWORK OF JOB DESCRIPTIONS

Job descriptions will include details of reporting relationships and then normally cover:

○ a statement of the overall purpose of the job;
○ a list of the main tasks or whatever other term is used.

Overall Purpose

The definition of the overall purpose of the job states in general terms what the job exists for – how it contributes to the achievement of the objectives of the team or department and, ultimately the mission and objectives of the organisation.

The definition of purpose should place the job in its setting within the organization and provide a basis for making an overall assessment of the job holder's contribution.

Main Tasks

The definitions of the main tasks the job holder is expected to undertake indicate the key result areas of the job. They spell out the areas in which job holders are accountable for the achievement of objectives, which wherever possible will be quantified as targets or expressed in the form of projects to be accomplished. In some cases it may not be able to attach quantified targets to the main tasks, in which case the task definition should provide the basis for deciding on the standard of performance the job holder is expected to reach.

The list of main tasks should cover all the key aspects of the job which together contribute to achieving its overall purpose. The number of task areas normally should be limited to seven or eight. There are very few jobs where more than that number is required and the whole job description should take up no more than the proverbial one side of one sheet of paper.

A main task definition starts with an active verb such as prepare, produce, plan, schedule, test, maintain, develop, monitor, ensure. It expresses specifically and succinctly (one sentence) *what* has to be done and *why* it has to be done. It does not try to explain *how* it is done. The statement of each task is written in the form: 'Do something in order to achieve a stated result or standard'. For example:

○ Prepare variance statements to keep production department managers informed of their expenditures in relation to budget.

○ Reply promptly to customer account enquiries.

○ Maintain stock records for bought-in parts.

○ Input changes to employee terms and conditions on to computerised personal record files.

In each of these cases the definition suggests a performance measure or indicator in the shape of a standard, for example:

○ Variance statements are produced accurately (no errors) and on time (within three days of the end of the accounting period).

○ Enquiries are processed with 24 hours.

○ Stock records are maintained 100 per cent accurately.

O Input changes are made promptly (within 24 hours) and 100 per cent accurately.

HOW TO PREPARE A JOB DESCRIPTION

When introducing performance appraisal it is probably best to abandon any existing job descriptions (which may be out of date anyhow) and start from scratch.

One way of preparing a job description is for the manager and the individual separately to answer a questionnaire and then meet to compare notes and resolve any differences between the answers. This has the advantage of bringing out into the open any misunderstandings about the job by either party and thus clears the way to a new agreed job description. Some skill will be required on the part of the manager to avoid confrontation and to handle the discussion in a way which leads to a conclusion with which both parties are satisfied.

A typical questionnaire addressed to an individual would cover the following points (the following example would also provide information for job evaluation purposes):

O What is your job title?

O To whom are you responsible?

O Who is responsible to you? (An organisation chart is helpful.)

O What is the main purpose of your job, ie in overall terms, what are you expected to do?

O To achieve that purpose, what are your main areas of responsibility?

O What is the size of your job in such terms of output or sales targets, numbers of items processed, numbers of people managed, number of customers?

O What targets or standards of performance have been defined for your job?

O Are there any other ways in which it would be possible to measure the effectiveness with which you carry out your job?

○ Is there any other information you can provide about your job to amplify the above facts such as:
— how your job fits in with other jobs in your department or elsewhere in the company;
— flexibility requirements in terms of having to carry out a range of different tasks;
— how work is allocated to you and how your work is reviewed and approved;
— your decision-making authority;
— the contacts you make with others, inside and outside the company;
— the equipment, plant and tools you use;
— other features of your job such as travelling or unsocial hours or unusual physical conditions;
— the major problems you meet in carrying out your work;
— the knowledge and skills you need to do your work?

The aim would then be to structure the discussion about the content of the job in line with these headings.

Although questionnaires like this can generate useful information, they are not essential. Much can be achieved simply by managers and individuals sitting down together and working through the following questions:

○ How would you describe the main purpose of your job?
○ What do you think are the most important things you have to do?
○ What do you believe you are expected to achieve in each of these areas?
○ How will you – or anyone else – know whether or not you have achieved them?

The answers to these questions may need to be sorted out – they can often result in a mass of jumbled information which has to be analysed so that the separate tasks can be distinguished and refined to seven or eight key areas. This process of job analysis and writing the task definition requires some skill which needs to be developed by training followed by practice.

The discussion should be as open as possible. The individual should be allowed the maximum scope to express his or her own views about the job. The manager can prompt and ask questions to clarify any information, but should not dominate the discussion. The aim is to get individuals to think for themselves about what they do. If they are given a reasonable amount of freedom to do so, they are much more likely to 'own' the result and will be more prepared to accept the use of the job description as a basis for appraisal.

Once the statement of main tasks has been agreed it will need to be updated as changes in responsibilities occur. The appraisal discussion provides a good opportunity for ensuring that this updating takes place.

Examples of job descriptions are given in Appendix A.

4

Defining Objectives, Competences and Values

Performance appraisal is very much about the management of expectations. These are defined and agreed under three headings:

1. As performance requirements expressed as objectives, the achievement of which is monitored by the use of agreed performance measures.
2. As competence requirements.
3. In the form of corporate values which job holders are expected to uphold.

OBJECTIVES

What Are Objectives?

An objective describes something which has to be accomplished – a point to be aimed at. Objectives or goals (the terms are interchangeable) define what organisations, functions, departments, teams and individuals are expected to achieve.

This definition sounds straightforward enough but more precision is required for performance appraisal purposes in defining the two main types of objectives and the different ways in which objectives can be expressed at corporate and individual levels.

Types of Objectives

There are two main types of objectives: work and developmental.

Work or operational objectives refer to the results to be achieved or the contribution to be made to the accomplishment of team, departmental and corporate objectives. At corporate level they are related to the organisation's mission, core values and strategic plans.

At departmental or functional level they are related to corporate objectives, spelling out the specific mission, targets and purposes to be achieved by a function or department.

At team level they will be related again specifically to the purpose of the team and the contribution it is expected to make to achieving departmental and corporate goals.

At individual level they are job-related, referring to the main activity areas or key tasks which constitute the individual's job. They focus on the results individuals are expected to achieve and how they contribute to the attainment of team, departmental and corporate goals and to upholding the organisation's core values.

Ideally, performance appraisal, especially when it is part of a performance management system, sets out not only to define objectives at each of these levels but also to integrate them so that a shared vision of performance requirements is created throughout the organisation, all contributing to the ultimate goal of organisational effectiveness and success. The ideal model of performance appraisal describes it as a shared process operated by high-involvement organisations with, in Charles Handy's words, 'a culture of consent'. In this model, objective-setting is not simply a top-down process which 'cascades' corporate objectives down through the organisation. Instead, there is an emphasis on participation in goal-setting to obtain commitment to corporate and team as well as individual objectives, and provision is made for an upward flow of contributions to the formulation of departmental and corporate objectives.

Developmental, ie personal or learning objectives, are concerned with what individuals should do and learn to improve their performance (performance improvement plans) and/or their knowledge and skills and competences (training and personal development plans). They are determined by means of appraisal discussions which establish any areas where improvement is required. These lead to performance agreements or plans which indicate what additional knowledge, enhanced skills or competences are needed to achieve objectives or work plans. Methods of analysing and defining skills and knowledge and competences are discussed later in this chapter.

A typical example of an objectives based approach to performance appraisal is provided by Pilkington Optronics. Seven or eight objectives are agreed, most of which are related to specific tasks or projects. Objectives are defined also for areas of general significance such as quality improvement. In addition, there will be a heading for personal or developmental objectives which spell out the areas in which the individual is expected to develop and improve his or her skills, knowledge and competences. The overall objectives are set for 12 months but there will be interim objectives or 'milestones' which will be reviewed quarterly.

How Are Individual Work Objectives Expressed?

Individual objectives define the results to be achieved and the basis on which performance in attaining these results can be measured. They can take the form of target or project-related objectives or standing objectives.

Target or Project-Related Objectives Individual objectives can be expressed as quantified output or improvement targets (open 24 new accounts by 31 December, reduce cost per unit of output by 2.5 per cent by 30 June) or in terms of projects to be completed (open distribution depot in Northampton by 31 October). Targets may be reset regularly, say once a year or every six months, or be subject to frequent amendments to meet new requirements or changed circumstances.

Standing Objectives Objectives for some aspects of a job (or for all aspects of some jobs) can be what might be described as 'standing objectives'. These are concerned with the permanent or continuing features of a job. They incorporate or lead to defined standards of performance which may be expressed in quantified terms such as the requirement to ensure that all deliveries are made within three days of receiving an order. Alternatively, they may have to be defined as qualitative standards such as:

> Performance will be up to standard if requests for information are dealt with promptly and helpfully on a can do/will do basis and are delivered in the form required by the user.

Qualitative standing objectives may also be defined for behaviour which will contribute to upholding the core values of the organisation as discussed in the last section of this chapter.

What is a good work objective?

Good work or operational objectives are:

○ *consistent*: with the values of the organisation and departmental and organisational objectives;

○ *precise*: clear and well-defined, using positive words;

○ *challenging*: to stimulate high standards of performance and to encourage progress;

○ *measurable*: they can be related to quantified or qualitative performance measures;

○ *achievable*: within the capabilities of the individual – account should be taken of any constraints which might affect the individual's capacity to achieve the objectives; these could include lack of resources (money, time, equipment, support from the manager or team leader or other people), lack of experience or training, external factors beyond the individual's control etc;

○ *agreed*: by the manager and the individual concerned – the aim is to provide for the ownership, not the imposition, of objectives, although there may be situations where individuals have to be persuaded to accept a higher standard than they believe themselves to be capable of attaining;

○ *time-related*: achievable within a defined time scale (this would not be applicable to a standing objective);

○ *teamwork oriented:* emphasise teamwork as well as individual achievement.

These requirements can be summed up by the acronym SMART to define a good objective:

S = stretching
M = measurable
A = agreed
R = relevant*
T = time related.

Defining Work Objectives

The process of agreeing objectives need not be unduly complicated. It should start from an agreed list of main tasks or what are sometimes referred to as principal accountabilities or key result areas. It is then simply a matter of jointly examining each area and agreeing targets and standards of performance as appropriate. Agreement can also be reached on any projects to be undertaken which might be linked to a specific accountability, or the agreement may refer to more general projects which fall broadly within the remit of the job holder.

Agreeing Main Tasks This should be done in accordance with the guidelines set out in the last chapter, namely:

○ Define the overall purpose of the job.
○ Identify the main tasks – not more than ten and covering all the different parts of the job which make a direct impact on achieving its overall purpose.
○ Use active verbs to define what is done in each area.
○ Define not only what has to be done but also why it has to be done.

---

* In this case R=relevant but note that in some contexts R=realistic.

Define Targets   The first step is to identify the key result areas of the job from the list of main tasks to which targets can be attached.

Targets are quantified and time-based – they always define specific and measurable outputs and when they have to be reached. The target may be to achieve a specified level of output or to improve performance in some way. Targets may be expressed in financial terms such as profits or sales to be made, income to be generated, costs to be reduced or budgets to be worked within. Or they may be expressed in numerical terms such as a specified number of units to be processed, responses to be obtained or clients or customers to be contacted over a period of time.

Targets define outputs but it should be remembered that these outputs are there to contribute to desired outcomes as expressed in the main task definition. There is, for example, no point in setting an output target for the number of calls per day or week a sales representative is expected to make unless outcome targets, in the shape of firm orders and sales value, are also defined.

Output targets are expressed in financial or some other quantified term, for example:

○ Achieve sales of £1.6m by 30 June.

○ Maintain inventory levels at no more than £12m.

○ Maintain throughput at the rate of 800 units a day.

Performance improvement targets may be expressed in terms such as:

○ Increase sales turnover for the year by 8 per cent in real terms.

○ Reduce the overhead to sales ratio from 22.6 to 20 per cent over the next 12 months.

○ Increase the ratio of successful conversions (enquiry to sales) from 40 to 50 per cent.

○ Reduce cost per unit of output by 3 per cent by the end of the year.

○ Reduce wastage rate to 5 per cent of stock by value.

O Achieve a 5 per cent improvement in customer ratings by the end of the year.

O Reduce the error rate to 1:1000 by 1 June

O Increase market share by 12 per cent within the next two years.

Define Performance Standards The next stage is to define performance standards for any main task to which specific time-based targets cannot be attached. These are sometimes described as standing or continuing objectives because, as explained earlier in this chapter, their essential nature may not change significantly from one review period to the next if the key task remains unaltered, although they may be modified if new circumstances arise.

Performance standards should have been broadly defined in outcome terms in the why part of the accountability/task definition. But the broad definition should be expanded and, as far as possible, particularised. Standards should preferably be quantified in terms, for example, of level of service or speed of response. Where the standard cannot be quantified a more qualitative approach may have to be adopted, in which case the standard of performance definition would in effect state: 'this job or task will have been well done if... (the following things happen)'. Junior or more routine jobs are likely to have a higher proportion of standing objectives to which performance standards are attached than senior and more flexible or output-oriented jobs.

The following are some examples of performance standards which spell out the end results required in quantitative terms:

O Prepare and distribute management accounts to managers within three working days of the end of the accounting period.

O Deal with 90 per cent of customer complaints within 24 hours – the remaining to be acknowledged the same day and answered within three working days.

O Hear job evaluation appeals within five working days.

○ Maintain a level of customer satisfaction in which complaints do not exceed 1:1000 transactions.

○ Acknowledge all customer orders within 24 working hours of receipt.

In each of these examples the figures expressing standards of performance may be changed occasionally, but the underlying objectives (levels of service, customer satisfaction, bad debt control, delivery to time, swift turnround of customer orders) are standing features of the job.

It may not always be possible to quantify performance standards as in the examples given above. The end results required may have to be defined in qualitative terms.

The fact that it is difficult or impossible to set quantifiable objectives for some jobs or segments of jobs does not mean that some form of measurement cannot take place. What can be done is to compare the results achieved in factual behavioural terms with the results expected, defined as standards of performance and also expressed in factual or behavioural terms.

It is often assumed that qualitative performance standards are difficult to define. But all managers make judgements about the standards of performance they expect and obtain from their staff, and most people have some idea of whether or not they are doing a good job. The problem is that these views are often subjective and are seldom articulated. Even if, as often happens, the final definition of a performance standard is somewhat bland and unspecific, the discipline of working through the requirements in itself will lead to greater mutual understanding of performance expectations and will facilitate the objective review of performance.

A performance standard definition should take the form of a statement that performance will be up to standard if a desirable, specified and observable result happens. This result could be defined in terms of:

○ achievement of already defined operational norms in such areas as administrative procedures, good employment practices, customer or client satisfaction and public image;

○ meeting already defined service delivery standards;

○ proportion of take-up of a service or facility;

○ change in the behaviour of employees, customers, clients or other people of importance to the organisation;

○ the reaction of clients, customers (internal and external) and outside bodies to the service provided;

○ the degree to which behaviour and performance supports core values in such areas as quality, care for people and teamworking;

○ speed of activity or response to requests;

○ ability to meet deadlines for 'deliverables';

○ existence of a backlog;

○ meeting defined standards of accuracy.

The following are some examples of qualitative performance standards:

○ Performance will be up to standard if line managers receive guidance on the interpretation and implementation of inventory policies which is acted on and makes a significant contribution to the achievement of inventory targets.

○ Performance will be up to standard when callers are dealt with courteously at all times, even when they are being difficult.

○ Performance will be up to standard if proposals for new product development are fully supported by data provided from properly conducted product research, market research and product testing programmes and are justified by meeting return on investment criteria policies.

○ Performance will be up to standard if the company's business plans are analysed and used to provide the basis for the realistic anticipation of future human resource requirements.

○ Performance will be up to standard if co-operative and productive relationships are maintained with fellow team members.

○ Performance will be up to standard if there is evidence of a sustained drive to improve quality standards.

○ Performance will be up to standard if it can be demonstrated that policies and programmes for continuous improvement have been implemented effectively and followed through for members of the department.

Define Projects   Projects may already have been defined as part of a team, departmental or functional plan; and when setting individual objectives it is simply necessary to agree on the part that the individual will play and the contribution he or she is expected to make. Alternatively, projects may be linked to one or more specific accountabilities or they may be related generally to the overall purpose of the job.

Objective setting for projects will specify the required outcome of the project (results to be achieved), its budget and its time-scale.

When a number of projects have to be undertaken by the job holder agreement should be reached on priorities.

Project or task achievement objectives may be expressed in terms such as:

○ Introduce new stock control system by 30 November.

○ All employees to have received training on the implementation of equal opportunities policies by 1 June.

○ New distribution centre to be operational by 1 March.

○ Reorganisation of finance department to be completed by 1 October.

For each project or task it would also be necessary to set out the success criteria, for example:

Introduce a new stock control system by 30 November to provide more accurate, comprehensive and immediate information on stock and thus enable inventory targets to be achieved without prejudicing production flows or customer service levels.

Agreeing Work Objectives

The agreement of work objectives is achieved by the manager and the individual getting together and answering the following questions:

○ What is the overall purpose of this job?

○ What are the main tasks which have to be carried out to achieve that overall purpose?

○ What corporate/functional/departmental objectives and values do we need to take into account in setting objectives for this job?

○ In what specific respects can this job contribute to the achievement of those objectives and upholding corporate values?

○ Taking each main task in turn, what, precisely, is the job holder expected to achieve expressed in the form of a target, a standard of performance or a project or special task to be completed as appropriate?

○ Are each of these objectives specific, measurable, agreed, realistic (achievable) and, where appropriate, time-related?

○ How are both the manager and the job holder going to know the extent to which the objectives have been achieved? (ie what are the performance measures or indicators?)

Difficulties in Agreeing Objectives

The agreement of objectives is not always straightforward. The following problems can arise:

○ It may be difficult to define specific and meaningful objectives.

○ Where quantified targets cannot be set it may be difficult to define qualitative standards and/or to identify appropriate performance indicators.

○ Individuals may not be prepared to accept the targets or standards their managers think should be set for their jobs.

○ Individuals may agree too readily to targets without thinking through how they are going to attain them and as a result may fail.

These problems can be avoided only by careful initial training and follow-up guidance and coaching if they still arise. This is an area where members of the human resources department can play a valuable part by providing help and advice.

Personal Objectives

Personal objectives emerge from the analysis and discussions which take place about the individual's performance compared with agreed work or operational objectives and the requirements for certain attributes (skill and knowledge) and levels of competence. The latter may be generic for all individuals in similar jobs or job families, or specific to the job holders.

The discussions will consider the factors which have contributed to achieving, meeting or failing to achieve objectives. These may be personal factors referring to the behaviour of the individual and the levels of skill or competence displayed, or external factors which may be outside the direct control of the individual but which he or she can reasonably be expected to manage.

In so far as the results obtained by individuals are attributable to the way in which they have carried out their work, training needs and areas of strength or weakness for development or improvement are established.

PERFORMANCE MEASURES

Measurement is a key aspect of performance appraisal on the grounds that 'if you can't measure it you can't improve it'. It is pointless to define objectives or performance standards unless there is agreement and understanding on how performance in achieving these objectives or standards will be measured.

Purpose of Measures

Performance measures should provide evidence of whether or not the intended result has been achieved and the extent to which the job holder has produced that result. This will be the basis for generating feedback information for use not only by managers but also by individuals to monitor their own performance.

The focus and content of performance measures will, of course, vary considerably between different occupations and levels of management.

Performance measures will work only if they are derived from clear main task definitions which focus on end results and suggest measurement. The definitions can indicate the measure to be used. For example, if one of the principal accountabilities of a sales manager is to develop new accounts, a target may be set to obtain 20 new customers within the next three months each of which generate sales of at least £15,000 a year. The performance measures of the number and the quality of the accounts are indicated in this target quite clearly.

However, the same sales manager may have a principal accountability which is to achieve and maintain a high degree of customer satisfaction. In this case measures of customer satisfaction would have to be agreed such as repeat or expanding business, absence of justifiable complaints, or response to a customer satisfaction survey. These measures may be quantified as targets or standards.

The performance measures for a factory manager might be summarised as follows:

1. Output – unit production figures and achievement of delivery deadlines.

2. Product quality – statistical quality control returns indicating variances outside specified limits; number of justified complaints on quality received from customers.

3. Productivity – output per employee; added value per employee.

4. Cost control – cost per unit of production; maintaining variances in standard costs within prescribed limits; keeping within overall agreed cost budgets; waste or scrap levels in relation to budget.

5. Stock control – ratio of inventory to current assets; achievement of agreed customer service levels; incidence of stockouts.

6. Utilisation of plant and machinery – percentage utilisation; amount of downtime.

7. Health and safety – accident frequency/severity rates; health and safety audit reports.

8. Employee relations – incidence of disputes and grievances; outcome of employee attitude surveys.

9. Employment – absenteeism and timekeeping figures; disciplinary actions and appeals.

10. Development – achievement of flexibility and multiskilling programmes.

Types of Measures

Performance measures may refer to such matters as income generation, sales, output, units processed, productivity, costs, delivery-to-time, 'take up' of a service, speed of reaction or turnround, achievement of quality standards or customer/client reactions.

Sun Life, for example, uses the three criteria of work quality, output and 'timeliness' (eg how many cases are dealt with over a given period of time). These are measured by a management information system.

Cambridgeshire County Council has identified four distinct types of measurement: money, time, effect and reaction.

O Money measures include maximising income, minimising expenditure and improving rates of return.

O Time measures express performance against work timetables, the amount of backlog and speed of activity or response.

O Measures of effect include attainment of a standard, changes in behaviour (of colleagues, staff, clients or customers), physical completion of the work and the level of take-up of a service.

O Reaction indicates how others judge the job holder and is therefore a less objective measure. Reaction can be measured by peer assessments, performance ratings by internal or external clients or customers or the analysis of comments and complaints.

Defining Performance Measures

It is important to agree performance measures at the same time as objectives are defined. This is the only way in which a fair assessment of progress and achievements can be made and the successful definition of performance measures will provide the best basis for feedback.

The following are guidelines for defining performance measures:

○ Measures should relate to results, not efforts.

○ The results must be within the job holder's control.

○ Measures should be objective and observable.

○ Data must be available for measurement.

○ Existing measures should be used or adapted wherever possible.

Performance Indicators

The terms performance measures and performance indicators are sometimes used interchangeably. Some organisations, however, distinguish between the two by reserving the term performance measures for results which can be quantified and performance indicators for situations when the outcome can only be judged more qualitatively on the basis of observable behaviour. For example, sales performance would be related to performance measures in the shape of sales turnover figures. However, the impact a job holder makes on other people would be related to a performance indicator which specifies the sort of reaction that the job holder should generate: 'Line managers express satisfaction with the promptness and accuracy of control information'.

The approach to defining performance indicators is similar to that used for performance measures as described above.

In practice, few organisations go to the trouble of trying to distinguish performance measures from indicators because this can result too easily in a distinction without a difference.

COMPETENCE ANALYSIS

A key feature of the new approach to performance appraisal as part of a performance management system is that it is concerned with inputs (competence) as well as outputs and outcomes (results and contribution). This is its main distinguishing feature from merit rating and traditional performance appraisal schemes which focused on inputs, and management by objectives which was almost exclusively related to outputs. A further distinguishing feature of the new approach to performance appraisal when compared with merit rating is that the assessment of levels of input is job or task related rather than concentrating on personality traits. Performance assessment is based on an understanding of the knowledge, skills, expertise and behaviour required to do a job well and on an analysis of the extent to which the attributes and behaviour of individuals meet defined criteria in each of these areas.

Competence analysis aims to define these criteria. In this respect, the analysis can be different from that carried out in defining main tasks and objectives. These are usually agreed specifically with individual job holders. Although there may be generic job descriptions, a proper approach to performance appraisal requires managers to discuss and agree key tasks on an individual basis. The same approach may and in many cases should be adopted for individual competence requirements, but the use of generic competences, ie those applying to a whole category of employees such as departmental managers, is more common.

What Are Competences?

The term competences refers to the behavioural dimensions of a role – the behaviour required of people to carry out their work satisfactorily. They constitute the behavioural characteristics which can be demonstrated to differentiate high performers in a given role under such headings as drive, achievement, team membership and management.

Competences are what people bring to a job in the form of different types and levels of behaviour. Competences govern the process aspects of job performance.

As more and more organisations adopt the language of competences, so they incorporate this concept in their performance appraisal systems. This has been the most powerful addition to this area over the last few years and has given a whole new language to the understanding, management and development of performance improvements.

The following is an example of a list of competences used by Standard Chartered in their performance appraisal scheme:

○ job and professional knowledge;

○ commercial/customer awareness;

○ communication;

○ interpersonal skills;

○ teamwork;

○ initiative/adaptability/creativity;

○ analytical skills/decision making;

○ productivity;

○ quality;

○ management/supervision;

○ leadership.

Generic and Specific Competences

Competences can be universally generic, applying to managers irrespective of which organisation they belong to, or their particular job. The list of competences drawn up by the Management Charter Initiative (MCI) comes into this category.

They can be organisationally generic, either general and applied to all staff, or focused more specifically on a job family or category of employees such as managers, scientists, professional staff or office/administrative staff. Alternatively, they may be defined for a job family hierarchy or, in some instances, all staff jobs, level by level. Competences also may be defined which are specific to individual roles.

Differentiating Competences

Differentiating competences define the behavioural characteristics which high performers display as distinct from those characterising less effective people – the performance dimensions for their job. The definitions of the level of competence expected of high performers in certain areas can be used as models for discussion at performance appraisal meetings.

One way of setting out the difference between high and less effective performers is to derive positive and negative indicators for each competence heading as in the following example for leadership.

Definition   Guiding, encouraging and motivating individuals and teams to achieve a desired result.

Positive Indicators
○ Achieves high level of performance from team.
○ Defines objectives, plans and expectations clearly.
○ Continually monitors performance and provides good feedback.
○ Maintains effective relationships with individuals and the team as a whole.
○ Develops a sense of common purpose in the team.
○ Builds team morale and effectively motivates individual members of the team by recognising their contribution while taking appropriate action to deal with poor performers.

Negative Indicators
○ Does not achieve high levels of performance from team.
○ Fails to clarify objectives or standards of performance.
○ Pays insufficient attention to the needs of individuals and the team.
○ Neither monitors nor provides effective feedback on performance.
○ Inconsistent in rewarding good performance or taking action to deal with poor performers.

Behaviourally Anchored Rating Scales (BARS)

Differentiating competences can be defined in the form of behaviourally anchored rating scales. For example, one performance dimension might be teamwork and a scale would be developed as follows:

1. Continually contributes new ideas and suggestions. Takes a leading role in group meetings but is tolerant and supportive of colleagues and respects other people's points of view. Keeps everyone informed about own activities and is well aware of what other team members are doing in support of team objectives.

2. Takes a full part in group meetings and contributes useful ideas frequently. Listens to colleagues and keeps them reasonably well informed about own activities while keeping abreast of what they are doing.

3. Delivers opinions and suggestions at group meetings from time to time but is not a major contributor to new thinking or planning activities. Generally receptive to other people's ideas and willing to change own plans to fit in. Does not always keep others properly informed or take sufficient pains to know what they are doing.

4. Tendency to comply passively with other people's suggestions. May withdraw at group meetings but sometimes shows personal antagonism to others. Not very interested in what others are doing or in keeping them informed.

5. Tendency to go own way without taking much account of the need to make a contribution to team activities. Sometimes uncooperative and unwilling to share information.

6. Generally uncooperative. Goes own way, completely ignoring the wishes of other team members and taking no interest in the achievement of team objectives.

Competence Analysis

Competence analysis provides the basis for producing competence profiles or models for use in performance appraisal and also selection and career development.

Competence analysis can be carried out by using the fairly complex and time-consuming methods of repertory grid or critical incident analysis. It can, however, be conducted quite satisfactorily by means of a structured interview, or a 'workshop' approach can be adopted in which a number of management 'experts' get together to analyse a job or a job family.

During the interview or workshop, the initial questions establish the overall purpose of the job and what it entails in terms of main tasks. It then goes on to analyse the behavioural characteristics which distinguish performers at different levels of competence.

The basic question is: 'What are the positive or negative indicators of behaviour which are conducive or non-conducive to achieving high levels of performance?' These may be analysed under such headings as:

O personal drive (achievement motivation);

O impact on results;

O analytical power;

O strategic thinking;

O creative thinking (ability to innovate);

O decisiveness;

O commercial judgement;

O team management and leadership;

O interpersonal relationships;

O ability to communicate;

O ability to adapt and cope with change and pressure;

O ability to plan and control projects.

In each area instances would be sought which illustrate effective or less effective behaviour.

Job Competency Assessment

An alternative approach is the job competency assessment method as described by L Spencer, D McClelland and S Spencer, *Competency Assessment Methods* (Hay/McBer Research Press,

1990) and which is based on David McClelland's research in what competency variables predict job performance. He established 20 competences which most often predict success. These are grouped into six clusters, as follows:

Achievement cluster

1. Achievement orientation.
2. Concern for quality and order.
3. Initiative.

Helping/service cluster

4. Interpersonal understanding.
5. Customer-service orientation.

Influence cluster

6. Impact and influence.
7. Organisational awareness.
8. Relationship building (networking).

Managerial cluster

9. Directiveness.
10. Teamwork and cooperation.
11. Developing others.
12. Team leadership.

Cognitive thinking/problem solving cluster

13. Technical expertise.
14. Information seeking.
15. Analytical thinking.
16. Conceptual thinking.

Personal effectiveness cluster

17. Self control, stress resistance.
18. Self-confidence.
19. Organisational commitment – 'business-mindedness'.
20. Flexibility.

McClelland then developed with his colleagues an expert system containing a database of competence definitions under the above headings.

The competency assessment method is used to model the competences for a generic job, ie a position occupied by a number of job holders where the basic duties are similar, such as research scientists in a laboratory or area sales managers. The method is based on McClelland's list of competences and uses the expert system developed from his research.

The starting-point is to assemble an expert panel of managers to express their vision of the job, its duties and responsibilities, any difficult job components, any likely future changes to the role and the criteria against which the job holder's performance is measured. The members of the panel nominate job holders whom they consider to be outstanding and those whom they consider satisfactory.

The next stage is to conduct a 'behavioural event interview' with the nominated job holders. This interview focuses on the distinction between a person's concepts about what it takes to be successful and what the person actually does to create that success. It employs a structured probe strategy, rather than a standard set of questions, to elicit what the interviewee sees as his or her most critical job experiences. The interview is investigative, not reflective, the object is to gather the most accurate performance data, not to collect a person's ideas about what he or she might have done under similar circumstances. The interviewees are not allowed to draw conclusions about what it takes to do that job, rather, they are pressed for information on their actual behaviour, thoughts and actions by a trained interviewer.

Following this analysis, differentiations can be made between superior and average performers in the form of:

O the competences that superior performers possess and exhibit which the average performers do not;

O the activities the average performers undertake which superior performers do not;

○ the competence and performance criteria that both superior and average performers exhibit, but the superior performers exhibit far more frequently.

Agreeing Individual Competences

If generic competence frameworks have not been prepared for the organisation it is still desirable for appraisers and appraisees to discuss what competences are required. It is not necessary to use the jargon. The discussion can simply focus on the following questions which could be discussed about each major aspect of the job:

○ What do we think needs to be done to ensure that this part of the job is performed well?

○ Can we think of any ways in which this task might be approached which would result in it not being done so well?

○ Can we now agree on the sort of behaviour in carrying out this task which is likely to produce good or poor results?

The aim would be to produce an agreement which would ensure that individuals understand the sort of behaviours expected of them and appreciate that if they fulfil these expectations they will be regarded as having performed well. In the following appraisal discussion reference can be made to specific results and examples of actual, observable behaviour in carrying out the task, and these could form the basis for assessing performance.

PERFORMANCE GUIDELINES

Another approach to defining expectations which is closely related to the competence approaches described above is the use of performance guidelines. A good example of the use of such guidelines is provided by the National Australia Group which has developed them for each of the major categories of employees in their banks. The guidelines are used in the appraisal discussion as the basis for assessing performance and for deciding any actions which may be necessary. An example of the guidelines for achievement and action is given in Figure 4.1.

VALUES

Increasingly, organisations are setting out the core values that they think should govern the behaviour of all their employees. Value statements may be produced which define core values in areas such as:

O care for customers;

O concern for people;

O competitiveness;

O enterprise;

O excellence;

O flexibility;

O growth as a major objective;

O innovation;

O market/customer orientation;

O performance orientation;

O productivity;

O quality;

O teamwork.

The individual statements may be backed up by lists of general principles on how they should be applied. For example, one of ICL's core values is commitment to teamwork. This commitment is defined as follows.

> Teamwork is vital to ICL because it improves our performance in two ways:
>
> 1. It helps to raise our individual standards by sharing talent and by improving each other's creative performance.
> 2. It enables everyone in our highly integrated business to work closely with others in order to harness all the skills the job requires.

ACHIEVEMENT AND ACTION

Focus on achieving results, keenness to 'get going and keep going'

Clerical	Supervisor	Manager	Senior manager	Executive
Seeks more responsibility within own work area and doesn't avoid or 'shelve' hard tasks	Seeks more responsibility within own work area and doesn't avoid or 'shelve' hard tasks	Is clear about what 'success' means for the business; resourceful in overcoming obstacles	Maintains focus on the 'bottom line' despite continuous changes to procedures and systems. Can maintain an 'operational' overview and be a good leader of people	Keeps focused on results, even when dealing with very diverse complex tasks and many different teams and projects. Can sustain this for long periods of time
Deals with problems as they happen – doesn't just wait to be told	Deals with problems as they happen – doesn't just wait to be told	Makes decisions without 'passing the buck' and sets personal performance standards	Accepts responsibility for poor as well as good team performance	Is proactive in tackling mistakes and is prepared to commit publicly to challenging targets
Looks for better ways of doing things	Looks for better ways of doing things	Takes early action to deal with problems even if it is difficult or unpopular	Acts constructively and positively, even when there are many uncertainties or a lot of opposition	Acts constructively and takes tough decisions. Works hard to get acceptance of those decisions even when they trigger high levels of conflict and personal criticism
Can be depended on to achieve results	Can be depended on to achieve results	Makes best use of resources to achieve outcomes	Makes long-term plans for a range of very different sorts of projects and activities	Develops action plans with very long timeframes even when there are unknowns or uncertainties associated with the project
High work output achieved	High work output achieved			
	Effective organisation and control of team and their work			

Figure 4.1 National Australia Group – example of performance guidelines

63

The guiding principles in developing teamwork are:

- Teamwork must be based on the need to heighten the capabilities, competences and contributions of each individual.
- Even when formal team structures do not exist, we have to get into the way of talking to each other and working together whenever it would improve performance to do so.

ICL accepts its obligations as a company to provide individuals with a high degree of freedom to do their job and to develop their own individuality and contribution to the full, within the context of real achievement through teamwork and cooperation.

Other organisations such as IBM have taken the critical core values and incorporated them in their 'contribution review system', the overall aim of which is to achieve 'market driven quality'. The system is based on an assessment of the contribution that it has been agreed employees should make to achieving the mission of their business unit or function. The emphasis is on self-assessment. An assessment is also made of performance in meeting continuing responsibilities – the basic ones all employees have for such matters as health and safety and BS 5750. Contributions are rated and these ratings influence pay decisions. In the IBM scheme, managers also meet to agree contribution rankings within groups of employees. The mandatory criteria used in ranking contribution are delivery, customer satisfaction and use of expertise (innovation and acquisition of skills). Others could include teamwork or 'prudent risk taking'.

The typical values which organisations incorporate into their appraisal schemes are:

○ customer service (internal as well as external);

○ teamwork;

○ (for managers) developing the performance of staff.

Definitions of the behaviour expected in upholding these values can be prepared for the organisation as a whole and individual appraisers would be required to discuss with appraisees the extent to which the latter's behaviour had supported the core value. This is an effective method of ensuring that espoused values are put into practice.

Part 3

CONDUCTING FORMAL APPRAISAL DISCUSSIONS

5

Conducting Appraisal Discussions – An Overview

Appraisal discussions enable a perspective to be obtained on past performance as a basis for making plans for the future. An overall view is taken of the progress made. Examples are used to illustrate that overview, and the analysis of performance concentrates not only on what has happened but also on why it has happened so that data is obtained for planning purposes. Obtaining historical perspective through analysis is a necessary part of an appraisal discussion but reaching agreement about what should be done in the future is what the discussion is really all about.

THE BASIS OF THE APPRAISAL DISCUSSION

The appraisal discussion provides the means through which the five key elements of performance appraisal can be achieved. These are:

1. **Measurement** – assessing results against agreed targets and standards.
2. **Feedback** – giving the appraisee information on how he or she has been doing.
3. **Positive reinforcement** – emphasising what has been done well so that it will be done even better in the future; only making constructive criticisms, ie those that point the way to improvement.
4. **Exchange of views** – ensuring that the discussion involves a full, free and frank exchange of views about what has been

achieved, what needs to be done to achieve more and what appraisees think about their work, the way they are guided and managed and their aspirations.

5. **Agreement** – jointly coming to an understanding about what has to be done by both parties to improve performance and overcome any work problems raised during the discussion.

KEY ASPECTS OF THE APPRAISAL DISCUSSION

When an appraiser and an appraisee get together they are there to engage in a dialogue about the appraisee's performance and development. This is not an interview in which one person asks the questions and the other provides the answers. It is more like a meeting in which views are exchanged so that an agreed conclusion can be reached.

Describing the formal appraisal meeting as a discussion implies that it is a free-flowing affair in which both parties are fully involved. This impression is correct, but it should not be assumed that the discussion should be allowed to meander to some inconclusive end. This is a conversation with a purpose; that purpose being to reach firm and agreed conclusions about the future development of the appraisee, any areas for improvement and how that improvement will be achieved. As such, the discussion has to be initiated with care and a variety of approaches and interpersonal skills are used to bring it to a successful conclusion.

There is no one right way of conducting an appraisal discussion – the approaches used will be strongly influenced by the circumstances, including the personalities and attitudes of the people involved. But there are a number of guidelines which should be taken into account by appraisers as summarised below and discussed in more detail in the next five chapters:

Preliminary phases

O Prepare carefully.

O Work to a clear but flexible structure.

O Create a supportive atmosphere.

General guidelines

O Let the appraisee do most of the talking.

O Encourage self-appraisal.

O Keep the whole year under review.

O No surprises – do not suddenly launch criticisms about past behaviour which should have been discussed at the time.

O Be positive, criticise constructively.

Using interpersonal skills

O Seek information by asking the right questions.

O Listen carefully.

O Be sensitive to the other person's concerns.

O Observe and respond to non-verbal signals.

O Maintain open, friendly body language.

O Be open to criticism.

O Test understanding.

O Reach agreement.

Completing the discussion

O Check understanding.

O Plan ahead.

O Rate performance, if that is part of the process.

O Complete documentation.

O End the meeting on a positive note.

6

Preliminary Phases

To get a performance appraisal discussion off to a good start it is necessary to:

O prepare carefully;

O set up a clear structure for the discussion;

O create a supportive atmosphere.

PREPARING CAREFULLY

A productive appraisal discussion depends upon careful and thorough preparation by both parties. The extent to which detailed preparation is needed will vary according to the type of meeting. More care would need to be taken for a formal annual discussion and the approach suggested below is aimed at such occasions. But the same principles would apply, albeit less formally, to interim appraisal discussions.

Preparation should be concerned with:

O setting up the meeting;

O what the appraiser should do to prepare for the meeting;

O what the individual should do to prepare for the meeting.

Setting Up The Meeting

If you are the appraiser it is a good idea to have a brief word with the appraisee some time (a week or two) before the discussion. If the performance appraisal scheme of your organisation has been properly introduced (see Chapter 15) appraisees should have been properly briefed about the purpose of the meeting and, ideally, should have received training in the part they will play. But it still helps to remind appraisees of why the discussion is taking place and the points that will be covered.

Explain that the purpose of the meeting is to give appraisees the opportunity to discuss with you how well they are doing. Say that, while the discussion will refer to performance and progress during the year and specific events will no doubt be mentioned, the emphasis will be on looking to the future rather than dwelling on the past. The aim will be to build up a total picture of where the appraisee has got to as a basis for deciding where he or she goes next. One of the principal aims of the meeting, you can stress, is to provide an opportunity for appraisees to talk about their future and the problems, if any, they are dealing with during the course of their work.

You can summarise by mentioning that the meeting will cover the following areas:

O a general review of progress;
O a discussion on future objectives and work and development plans;
O a discussion on any point which appraisees wish to raise.

Your aim should be, as far as possible, to emphasise the positive nature of the process and to dispel any feelings of trepidation on the part of appraisees. You should be attempting to put them in the right frame of mind to prepare for the discussion along the lines described below.

Preparation By The Appraiser

If you are the appraiser, it is a good idea to consider the points you want to bring out in the discussion in advance, and you will need to support these points with examples of good or poor results or effective or ineffective behaviour. It is helpful to make notes during the year on what has gone particularly well or particularly badly for this purpose. You can bring out these observations during your discussions with appraisees to show that you have really noticed and appreciated their work as well as to substantiate with chapter and verse any adverse comments you have to make. But use them with care; the appraisal discussion is not the time to rake over everything that has happened since the last formal meeting. The discussion should be regarded as essentially a stocktaking exercise in which factual evidence may be used to support overall conclusions on progress made during the year.

The basis for preparation should be the established job and competence requirements. These will have been extended and further defined by any specific targets, standards, projects and plans that were agreed at the last formal discussion (often called a 'performance agreement'), subject to any revisions that have been made to them during the year. Reference should also be made to any notes made during or following interim appraisal discussions about appraisee's performance. Changes in the appraisee's role since the last review should be noted. Consideration should be given to any changes in internal organisational, divisional or departmental circumstances and priorities which have taken place since the last formal discussion. External pressures which may have affected results should also be noted.

You should then work your way through the following checklist of questions:

Performance analysis

1. How well do you think the appraisee has done in achieving his/her objectives during the review period?
2. How well have any improvement, development or training plans as agreed at the last review meeting been put into effect?
3. Are there any aspects of the appraisee's performance (be specific) which deserve particular praise and should be mentioned during the discussion?
4. Are there any aspects of the appraisee's performance (be specific) which you think should be criticised in the appraisal discussion?

5. What approach are you going to adopt to ensure that your criticisms are constructive (ie they lead to plans to overcome the problem) and are accepted by the appraisee?
6. What are the factors which you think may have affected the performance of the appraisee? (Consider both factors over which the appraisee had control and factors which were beyond his or her control.)
7. Can you think of any particular events or observed behaviours which you think may have influenced the results achieved?

Support for the appraisee

8. Are you satisfied that you have given the individual sufficient guidance or help on what he/she is expected to do? If not, what extra help/guidance could you provide?
9. Are you satisfied that the appraisee has the amount of resources and authority required to carry out the work effectively? If not, what are you going to do about it?

Development needs

10. Are there any areas where knowledge or skills or levels of competence need to developed?
11. Is there any additional experience from which the appraisee would benefit?

The appraisee's present and future

12. Is the best use being made of the appraisee's skills and abilities? If not, what should be done?
13. Is the appraisee ready to take on additional responsibilities in his/her present job? If so, what?
14. Do you think the appraisee and the organisation would benefit if he/she were provided with further experience in other areas of work?
15. What direction do you think the individual's career could take within the organization?

Content of performance agreement

16. What changes do you think are required to the appraisee's job description arising from any past or projected changes in job requirements?

17. What objectives relating to the individual's main tasks would you like to agree with him/her for the next period?

18. What sort of work and performance improvement plans would you like to discuss with the appraisee to ensure that job requirements and objectives are achieved?

19. What specific development or training does the individual need to help in his/her work and/or to further his/her career with the organisation?

20. What action do you need to take personally to give the appraisee additional training or guidance, to clarify accountabilities or to ensure that he/she has the resources and authority required to do the work effectively?

Preparation By The Appraisee

It can be suggested to appraisees that it is equally desirable for them to consider their achievements and any problems they have met in reaching their objectives as a basis for the discussion, especially as you will be giving them an opportunity to talk about how they have been doing and where they want to go from there. It is probably best to avoid a too pointed reference to 'self-appraisal' which is jargon and may put people off as sounding too much like an invitation to sit in a confessional box.

Appraisees can be provided with a checklist such as the example given below to help them think about the points which will be raised in the discussion.

Appraisee's preparation checklist

1. Taking each part of my job description in turn, how well have I carried out that aspect of my work?

2. To what extent have I achieved the objectives I agreed at my last appraisal discussion?

3. In what aspects of my work have I been most successful (give examples) and why?

4. Are there any aspects of my work where I have not done as well as I would wish (give examples) and why?

5. Would I have benefited from better guidance, help and training from my manager/team leader? If so, what form should it take?

6. Are there any specific aspects of my work where there may be some room for improvement? If so, what am I going to do about them?

7. Are there any changes needed to my job description to reflect changing responsibilities?

8. What objectives should be set for each of the main aspects of my job (my key result areas) for next year?

9. What steps do I think will be necessary to ensure that these objectives are achieved?

10. What ideas have I got about my future in this organisation?

WORK TO A CLEAR BUT FLEXIBLE STRUCTURE

Every appraisal discussion is a unique occasion and must be planned and conducted in accordance with the needs and personalities of both parties. It is inappropriate to have a rigid agenda and the discussion should be conducted flexibly. More time may be needed on some aspects than others and the original order which the appraiser had in mind may have to be changed. The discussion should not be over-formalised. But it is necessary to ensure that all the points that need to be covered are dealt with and it is therefore useful to have some basic framework in mind although the discussion may proceed flexibly within that framework. A typical outline for a discussion would look like this:

1. A review of each element in the job description, discussing what has gone well and what has gone less well, and why.

2. A point-by-point examination of the results of the objectives and actions agreed at the last meeting.

3. A discussion and agreement on the performance objectives for the next period in the shape of targets and standards of performance.

4. A discussion and agreement on the appraisee's developmental objectives.

5. A discussion and agreement on the actions to be taken to ensure that the performance and developmental objectives are achieved.

6. A general discussion of any other matters of concern, including the appraisee's aspirations.

7. A check that there is mutual understanding of the objectives and action plans.

An alternative approach would be to structure the discussion around a preparation form to be completed in advance by the appraisee containing questions such as those listed above.

CREATING THE RIGHT ATMOSPHERE

It is no good appraisers hauling appraisees into their offices without any warning, plonking them down in front of their formidable desks, firing a battery of questions and criticisms at them for 20 minutes or so and then quickly ticking the boxes in the form provided by the personnel department.

Appraisers may feel they have done their duty by completing this onerous task as required by personnel, but they will have failed utterly to take advantage of a real opportunity to motivate their staff to improve performance, thus helping the appraisers to achieve their own objectives. Instead, they will probably have succeeded in thoroughly demotivating their staff.

This may appear to be an exaggeration but all too often it happens this way. Research has shown that in many organisations managers go through a ritual of appraisal as laid down by the personnel department with the result that appraisees are more likely to be demotivated than motivated by the process.

If you are the appraiser you must remember that appraisees often are nervous, even frightened, of appraisal discussions which they perceive as occasions when they will be at the receiving end of criticism and blame. If they are not nervous, they may well be cynical. They have seen it all before and believe that their managers are simply going through the motions.

To conduct a successful appraisal discussion you must be aware of these fears or attitudes and take the following steps to create an informal environment in which a full, frank but friendly exchange of views can take place.

Prior Information

As mentioned above, let the appraisee know some time in advance that you want to hold an appraisal discussion, emphasising that this will be an informal exchange of views which will concentrate mainly on the future – building on, or at least aiming at, success.

The appraisee also should be asked to prepare for the discussion using a checklist such as the example given earlier in this chapter. You can suggest that the appraisee make notes on any points to be brought up during the discussion. In some organisations the appraisee is asked to complete a preparation form such as the one illustrated in Appendix B. If such a form is used, however, it is preferable not to ask the appraisee to give it to the appraiser in advance as this would probably prejudice the atmosphere of freedom and spontaneity which is an essential requirement for a fruitful appraisal discussion. Preparation forms should only be used as *aides mémoire*. It is sufficient for appraisers to know the areas which the appraisee will be covering, including the fact that appraisees will be invited to make comments about the quality of guidance and support provided by their appraisers. This is a form of upward appraisal and helps appraisers to get the maximum benefit from the discussion in that it provides them with an extra dimensional view of how well they are performing as managers.

Timing

The interview should be timed to take place on a date and at a time which is convenient to both parties. Neither the appraiser nor the appraisee should be unduly pressed for time and neither of them should be too preoccupied with other issues. The appraisal discussion should be perceived as an event which is as important as any other aspect of the work of both the appraiser and the appraisee. At the end of the discussion neither party should say or think: 'I can now get back to my *real* work'.

At least an hour should be allowed for the discussion – more for complex jobs. But two hours is probably as much time as can usefully be spent. The discussion might have to be reasonably exhaustive but it should never be exhausting.

Every effort should be made to ensure that the discussion is not interrupted. You should not be late for the appointment or keep the appraisee waiting.

Opening The Discussion

You should not sit behind your desk to conduct the discussion. If you do, the desk will act as a barrier and inhibit the free exchange of information and ideas which is essential to its success. The best position is for the appraiser and the appraisee to sit not quite opposite to one another, with at most a low table between them, on which papers can be placed.

Starting

The first thing to do is to put the appraisee at ease. Start with some fairly general comments before plunging into detail. It is clearly highly undesirable to hit the appraisee with critical comments at the outset. Your aim should be to build up good trust levels during the discussion. Unless these exist, appraisees will not be sufficiently free from anxiety to participate willingly, to undertake honest self-appraisal and to play a full part in problem-solving dialogues. Obviously, this will be far easier to achieve if a trusting relationship has been established already on a day-to-day basis between you and the appraisee. The process will be further enhanced if the culture of the organisation engenders mutual trust between management and employees. If, however, the relationship between the appraiser and the appraisee is usually distant, even cold, it may be much more difficult to establish good rapport during an appraisal discussion. In fact, a sudden switch into a different mode of behaviour might get the whole meeting off to a false start. Appraisers cannot and should not try to become different people, but they can still try to get a productive dialogue going in the appraisal discussion by adopting the following approach:

○ Start by reminding the appraisee of the purpose of the discussion, stressing that this is not to dwell unduly on the past but to look to the future.

○ Let the appraisee know how much time you have set aside for the discussion to demonstrate that you are not going to rush through it.

○ Continue by explaining that the aim is to come to an agreement on what has been achieved since the last meeting and what is to be achieved in the future.

○ This should be followed by a brief exchange in which each party itemises the key points they want to discuss – setting the agenda.

○ The discussion can then begin, probably with an invitation from the appraiser for the appraisee to talk generally about the progress he or she has been making during the year by reference to notes made prior to the meeting or a completed preparation form. This could be initiated by a fairly general, open question along the lines of: 'Would you like to tell me about how you think you have been getting on since our last appraisal discussion?' It may be necessary to follow up this open question with more probing questions to elicit specific responses, but the initial general question should at least start the ball rolling. This approach of inviting self-appraisal is discussed in more detail in the first section of the next chapter.

7

General Guidelines

There are a number of general guidelines on how the appraisal discussion may be conducted and these are described in this chapter. Each of them should be interpreted and applied according to the circumstances in which the discussion is taking place and the personalities of those involved – there is no one right way to conduct an appraisal discussion.

LET THE APPRAISEE DO MOST OF THE TALKING

During the discussion you will be seeking information from the appraisee. To do this you must encourage them to do most of the talking.

If you are the appraiser remember that it is the appraisee's meeting as well as yours. Appraisal is not something that a manager does to a subordinate. It is rather something that they do together. Getting appraisees to participate fully is vital to the success of the discussion. If you give appraisees plenty of time to talk through the issues and put forward their own solutions to problems you are much more likely to obtain willing agreement to revised objectives and performance improvement plans. Ownership will only be achieved through involvement.

Reinforce the fact that you want to hear their views and that you are going to work together to iron out any problems which have been met in carrying out work. Throughout the discussion put the onus on the appraisee to make the running. Ask appraisees to expand on any comments they make about their achievements, and suggest that they give examples. After you have given them that opportunity add your own comments and discuss the issues generally.

You can encourage appraisees to participate by asking the right questions and then actively listening to the answers. The inter-personal skills you can use in these aspects of the discussion are described in Chapter 9. When appraisees have responded to your invitation to participate, you may need to do no more than reflect the points they have made and summarise them before going on to the next part of the discussion.

Remember that the more top-down you are, the more auto-cratic you are, the less you ask for involvement, participation and feedback from the appraisee, then the less the discussion is going to be about learning. It is going to be about telling, and the trouble with telling people is that as a result we do not know what has been learned. Essentially, the appraisal discussion is about:

○ the appraisee's learning;
○ where they have got to;
○ where they are going;
○ how they are going to get there;
○ how they feel about things;
○ what they feel able to do.

ENCOURAGE SELF-APPRAISAL

One way of getting participation is to encourage self-appraisal. This means getting individuals to analyse and assess their own performance as a basis for discussion. In previous chapters it was mentioned that this is often carried out prior to the appraisal discussion, and the notes made in response to a checklist or a completed pre-appraisal form can be used as an agenda for the meeting.

Research has shown that when an element of self-appraisal is incorporated, the appraisal process is likely to generate less inhib-ited and more positive discussion and to provide a better climate for identifying problems, considering solutions and helping individuals to realise their potential and develop their career prospects. Self-appraisal can reduce defensiveness by encouraging appraisees to take the lead in reviewing their own performance, rather than having an assessment imposed on them, and it focuses their attention on the key performance and development issues with which they should be concerned.

The advantages of self-appraisal were summed up by Gordon Anderson (*Managing Performance Systems*, Blackwell, 1993) as follows:

○ It overcomes many of the traditional problems of performance appraisal by improving the flow of relevant accurate information to appraisers.

○ It assists in resolving uncertainties about criteria for job success.

○ It is likely to reduce defensive behaviour.

○ It can have a positive effect on employee motivation by involving employees in an active way in the appraisal process.

○ It encourages better preparation for appraisal interviews.

○ It helps to develop more positive attitudes to performance appraisal.

○ It generates a proactive approach to development.

Even when a self-appraisal form has not been completed before the meeting you can still initiate the discussion by asking such questions as:

○ How do you feel you have done?

○ What are you best at doing?

○ Are there any parts of your job which you find difficult?

○ Are there any aspects of your work in which you feel you would benefit from better guidance or further training?

But there are a number of issues which need to be addressed if self-appraisal is to succeed. First, appraisees must have clear standards and targets against which they can measure their performance.

Second, there has to be a high level of mutual trust between the appraisers and appraisees. The latter must believe that their appraisers will not take advantage of an honest self-appraisal. Research has shown that the greater the extent to which appraisers adopt the role of helper and show that they value and respect appraisees as people, the greater the likelihood of a trusting relationship being developed, especially if this approach is adopted throughout the year and is not just turned on during the annual appraisal discussion.

Third, under-confident individuals may feel that self-appraisal is a sort of test of themselves, and appraisers have to ensure that they understand this is not the case. Finally, some people believe that self-appraisal means that employees will overestimate their performance, which leaves the manager in the awkward situation of having to cut them down to size. But the experience of most organisations that introduce self-appraisal is that appraisees are more likely to underestimate themselves and this provides appraisers with a splendid opportunity to boost their confidence. Even if there is an element of over-valuation this at least gives appraisers the chance to put the record straight, as long as they adopt a tactful approach and use actual examples to illustrate the points they want to make.

KEEP THE WHOLE PERIOD UNDER REVIEW

Both appraisers and appraisees should keep the whole period under review. They should not refer just to recent events. It is a great temptation to concentrate on the most obvious successes or failures in the weeks before the appraisal discussion. They are, after all, fresh in their minds and are making the most impact on current results. But the appraisal discussion should aim to produce a fully rounded survey of performance and this cannot happen if two-thirds of the year or more are ignored. It is worth repeating the point that the purpose of the historical part of the discussion is to obtain an overview of the main performance issues as a prelude to the much more important forward-looking aspects of the meeting.

NO SURPRISES

Do not deliver unexpected criticisms – there should be no surprises. The focus of the discussion should reflect the day-to-day contacts between the appraiser and the appraisee. The discussion should be concerned only with events or behaviours which have been noted at the time they take place. Feedback on performance should be immediate and continuous and as far as possible should be built into the job. It should not wait until the end of the year. The function of the initial, retrospective, section of the formal appraisal discussion is to take an overall view of performance over the year and on this basis to look ahead.

If you do spring something on appraisees during the discussion their immediate reaction is likely to be 'This is the first I've heard of this, why didn't you tell me at the time?', and this will seriously prejudice the likelihood of a productive discussion.

RECOGNISE ACHIEVEMENTS AND REINFORCE STRENGTHS

Where possible you should begin with praise for some specific achievement. The accent in appraisal should be on praise. Everyone needs encouragement and appreciation, and praise helps people to relax in what are potentially the sticky moments at the start of an appraisal discussion. However, praise must be sincere and deserved. It is no good simply going through the motions. You must refer to actual achievements and spell out the contribution made to the success of the team or department.

It is possible to be mechanical about praise. There was an American training film for sales managers which promoted the formula 'two pats on the back for every kick on the ass'. Appraisees can see through this approach and reject the praise as insincere. Even if you dress it up a bit more carefully than this you could still produce negative results. The following sequence is not untypical:

O Objective number one: fantastic.

O Objective number two: that was great.

O Objective number three: that could not have been done better.

O Now objective number four: this is what we really need to talk about, what went wrong?

If this sort of approach is adopted, the discussion will focus on the failure, the negatives, and the appraisee will become defensive. This can be destructive and explains why some people fear the annual appraisal discussion as something which is likely to turn into a 'beat me over the head session', only taking place as a means to generate evidence for disciplinary action.

As Professor Clive Fletcher notes in *Appraisal: Routes to Improved Performance* (Institute of Personnel and Development, 1993):

> Be sure to give full recognition to the appraisee's achievements and strengths; note specific examples of good work. It is particularly helpful to express appreciation of tasks which have not come easily and which have called for real effort or persistence on the individual's part.

Your aim should be to reinforce strengths not to undermine them. Reinforcement takes place when successful behaviour is rewarded with recognition and praise and individuals are therefore more likely to repeat the behaviour in the future because they expect to be rewarded for it. This is non-financial motivation which can have a deeper and longer-lasting impact on performance than financial motivation through a performance-related pay system. People are more likely to be motivated and feel committed to achieving higher levels of performance if they feel valued. Obviously, pay is the clearest indication of the value attached by the organisation to individuals and this is why it is so important to get the reward system right. But the direct impact of an increase in pay, as Herzberg established in *The Motivation to Work* (Wiley, 1957), is not likely to last long and can be positively demotivating if individuals feel that the performance-related pay increase is inadequate (as it often is) or the pay system is inequitable. Herzberg regarded pay as a 'hygiene' factor. You must get it right but it prevents dissatisfaction rather than creates long-range satisfaction. The main 'satisfiers' in Herzberg's terms, are achievement, recognition and responsibility. All these can be influenced by managers, who often have little power to make pay decisions, and the appraisal discussion provides an excellent opportunity for exerting that influence.

In reviewing performance over the year you may have to refer to mistakes. However, you should make the point that anyone can make mistakes and occasional failures are inevitable in trying to reach really tough targets. What you should also emphasise, however, is that you expect appraisees to learn from their mistakes so that they do not repeat them, and you should consider with them ways in which over the next period new targets can be achieved, however stretching they may be.

CRITICISE CONSTRUCTIVELY

Praise is important but the appraisal discussion must also cover those aspects of performance which have not met expectations, tackling any issues which arise because objectives have not been achieved. It is easy enough to say 'well done' to people – to pass on the good news. It is often much harder to continue with 'and now the bad news'. Managers often are reluctant to criticise because it makes them uncomfortable, or they fear a hostile and defensive reaction, they want to retain their 'nice' image.

This reluctance may have been influenced by the 'softer' approaches to management popularised over the last few decades. The worst excesses of the human relations and behavioural science movements in this respect may have been discredited but there is still a strong residual climate in favour of just being nice to people. Even books like these which emphasise the positive nature of performance appraisal can be wrongly interpreted as recommending that appraisers should only focus on the good points. It is just as important to be positive about weaknesses as about strengths in the sense of analysing and under-standing them as a basis for future action.

Those engaged in the fashionable pursuit of empowerment can fall into this trap. They emphasise the soft part of its philoso-phy which says: 'enrich people's jobs, push decisions downwards closer to the point of impact, trust people rather than assume they will cheat you'; but they pay insufficient attention to the hard part. Empowerment involves a greatly increased emphasis on holding individuals to account for what they do, and on continuous improvement. This means that people are not only expected to put right those things which have gone badly but also to learn from their mistakes or failures and do better. Ideally, they should recognise these problems themselves. In practice, managers must have the strength of mind and purpose to ensure that their staff know when things have gone wrong and to place them in a position to do better next time. Self-generated feed-back is a highly desirable feature of performance appraisal but there will always be a need for managers to provide negative as well as positive feedback based on their own observations and understanding.

Most individuals appreciate high quality feedback – they like to know where they stand. They want to know when they have done well and when it is thought they have not done so well, if only, in the latter case, to have the opportunity of putting the record straight.

A performance appraisal discussion without any criticisms would be regarded by many individuals as suspect – there are very few people around who really believe that they have performed consistently at the highest level in all aspects of their jobs. They accept that they may get negative as well as positive feedback. However, research has shown that most people can cope with, and do something about, criticisms of two or three aspects of their performance but no more.

If any aspects of performance have to be criticised this must be done constructively. This means being certain that it is the performance that is being criticised not the individual. The criticism should not be perceived as an end in itself. The objective of criticism is to bring about positive changes in behaviour. Thus it is vital to make the point, get a response and go straight into planning how to bring about changes.

Clive Fletcher (ibid) believes that when tackling performance weaknesses you should remember that they may be aspects of a person's performance that are only weak in comparison with that individual's overall performance and not weak in comparison with other people. If this is the case, you should point it out to the appraisee saying, in effect, that your aim is to help the good to become better.

The following methods of handling criticism have been suggested by Professor Fletcher (ibid):

O Let appraisees know that you appreciate their frankness in identifying any shortcomings.

O Get appraisees to produce their own ideas on remedial action.

O Provide appraisees with reassurance if they mention an aspect of their performance which falls below their own standards but you think is satisfactory.

O If appraisees do not agree that there is a problem, be firm but specific, giving examples.

O Confine your comments to weaknesses that can be put right, do not try to alter the appraisee's personality.

O Do not tackle more than two weaknesses in one meeting – there is a limit to how much criticism individuals can take without becoming defensive.

Constructive criticism involves helping people to help themselves but if they come up with impractical or irrelevant proposals you have to step in tactfully and guide them towards a better solution. This will be easier if you concentrate on what needs to be done to deal with specific problems arising from a failure to achieve objectives as established in the analytical processes described earlier in this chapter.

Essentially, constructive criticism is about being positive. In the words of the old song, your approach as an appraiser should be to 'to accentuate the positive and eliminate the negative'. The emphasis should always be on looking forward, on managing success.

Eliminating the negative does not, of course, mean that you avoid mentioning any issues of substandard performance. What you can do is to turn a negative into a positive by not simply blaming appraisees for going wrong but by helping them to appreciate what they should do, possibly with your help, to put things right.

Thus you do not say: 'I see that you failed to meet the target for turning round enquiries; you must do better than that next year'. Instead, you say: 'What can we do to ensure that you meet your enquiry turnround target?' You are there to establish the facts – it will not be productive to say: 'You shouldn't have done that', it is better to say 'Why did you do that?' and then move on to address the problem together.

ADOPT A JOINT PROBLEM-SOLVING APPROACH

In this approach, you abandon the role of judge and become a helper. Your appraisal is not handed down to the appraisee – instead a discussion takes place about any work problems the appraisees have. They are encouraged to think through their own solutions to them, including any changes in their own behaviour to achieve improvement. You must ensure that appraisees make suggestions which are both realistic and practical and that they do take on the responsibility for undertaking the actions required, with your help where necessary. But you do not simply tell them that they have got it wrong. Instead you encourage people to think it out for themselves by questioning them:

O How do you propose to do this?

O What are the specific steps you think you will have to take?

O Do you think you will meet any problems in getting this done?

O What would you do if you found that you were not getting the information you needed on time?

The 'What if...?' approach is often fruitful as a means of generating ideas as well as of exploring the practicality of a proposed course of action. Ask questions such as:

O *What if* we approached production control jointly to see if they can provide you with more up-to-date information on potential delays? How should we tackle them?

O *What if* we had a look at the filing system to see if we can simplify it? What would that mean in practical terms?

O *What if* we called a meeting of your most important internal clients to get their ideas on what sort of service they want from you? How would you approach such a meeting?

Appraisees may not always volunteer suggestions and you may have to prompt them. If this fails to work, point out what sort of behaviour you believe is desirable. If this should be the case, you should be descriptive of the behaviour you expect: 'You tend not to make many comments in meetings; you *have* something to contribute and it would be constructive to voice your opinion'. Remember to deal with behaviour that the appraisee can change, not 'You shouldn't be so shy'.

To sum up, the emphasis should be on the consideration of how difficulties can be overcome, not simply on handing out to appraisees evaluative criticisms of past performance, although the joint analysis of the reasons why performance has not matched expectations will point the way to plans for improvement. Approaches to performance analysis are discussed in the next chapter.

8

Performance analysis

It has been pointed out a number of times earlier in this book that the appraisal discussion is essentially a forward-looking affair, a dialogue about what can be done to develop skills and competences and what steps need to be taken to improve performance so that even better results are achieved in the future.

This aim, however, can only be achieved by analysing current and recent performance. The value of performance appraisal, when it is conducted properly, is that it is related to real situations and actual events which indicate what needs to be done. The analysis should concentrate on performance, not personality, and it involves:

O analysing performance in relation to objectives;
O assessing the reasons for good or less good performance and agreeing on how strengths can be developed or the extent to which any shortcomings have arisen from lack of knowledge or skills or failure to achieve acceptable levels of competence;
O providing feedback.

These aspects of performance analysis are discussed in the rest of this chapter.

ANALYSE PERFORMANCE NOT PERSONALITY

One of the wisest management thinkers, Douglas McGregor, pointed out in his article 'An uneasy look at performance appraisal' (*Harvard Business Review*, May–June, 1957) that: 'Managers are uncomfortable when they are put in the position of playing God'. He went on to suggest that the emphasis should be shifted from the appraisal of personality to the analysis of performance. He wrote:

> This implies a more positive approach. No longer is the subordinate being examined by the superior so that his (sic) weaknesses may be determined; rather he is examining himself, in order not only to define his weaknesses but also his strengths and potentials... He becomes an active agent, not a passive 'object'. He is no longer a pawn in a chess game.

He went on to say that if the accent of the review is on performance, on actions relative to goals:

> There is less tendency for the personality of the subordinate to become an issue. The superior, instead of finding himself in the position of a psychologist or therapist, can become a coach, helping the subordinate to reach his own decisions on the specific steps that will enable him to reach his targets.

What Douglas McGregor wrote all that time ago has had considerable influence on current best practice in performance appraisal. It is agreed by all commentators that discussions on performance should be based on fact, not opinion. Appraisers should always refer to actual events or behaviour and to results compared with agreed objectives. Appraisees should be given plenty of time to explain why something did or did not happen.

As an appraiser, your job is to focus on what appraisees have done, not the sort of persons they are. You may be able to influence appraisees to change their behaviour but you are most unlikely to succeed in getting them to change their personality. In any case, if you say or imply that, for example, a person is too introverted, or is emotionally unstable or lacks integrity, you will get nowhere. All that will happen is a negative or defensive reaction from the appraisee. This could take the form of 'fight or flight', a hotly expressed rejection of your views or a sullen retreat into negative behaviour. Your concern is not with the personalities of appraisees, it is what they do with their personalities that counts, and you can influence that. And this means first finding out what they have done and then exploring the reasons for any successes or failures.

ANALYSE PERFORMANCE IN RELATION TO AGREED OBJECTIVES

Performance analysis will always be more meaningful if it is done by reference to agreed objectives and performance measures. These provide a proper factual basis and the evidence required to discuss achievements and to criticise constructively.

The following questions need to be answered when reviewing achievements against objectives:

1. Were the objectives 'SMART' ie stretching, measurable, accepted, relevant and time related?
2. Have any circumstances arisen since the objectives were originally agreed that make them irrelevant or unattainable?
3. Are the available performance measures appropriate?
4. To what extent have targets been reached or performance standards attained?
5. Is there reliable evidence to support this view?
6. What specific actions or behaviours of the appraisee have contributed to success or failure in achieving objectives?
7. To what extent have the actions or behaviour of the appraisee's manager or team leader helped or hindered the attainment of objectives?
8. Are there any circumstances entirely beyond the control of the appraisee which have prevented him or her achieving objectives?
9. What changes need to be made to existing objectives?
10. What needs to be done in the future to ensure that objectives will be reached?

It is vital that these questions should be addressed jointly by the appraiser and the appraisee. The aim should be to achieve agreement under each heading, so that appraisees accept the findings of the performance analysis and 'own' the solution to any problems which have emerged. To do this, appraisers must deploy a number of interpersonal skills as described in the next chapter.

ANALYSING REASONS FOR GOOD OR NOT SO GOOD PERFORMANCE

Good performance should not be taken for granted. Reinforcement is necessary so that the appraisee continues to deliver even better results. Therefore, it is useful to discuss exactly why things went well so that successes can be repeated.

If, however, there have been shortcomings or failures the reasons for these must be established so that action can be taken to avoid their re-occurrence. What you need to determine is the extent to which the reason for the problem is because the appraisee:

1. Did not receive adequate support or guidance from you.
2. Did not fully understand what he/she was expected to do.
3. Would not do it – attitude.
4. Did not know how to do it – knowledge or skill.
5. Could not do it – competence.

The solutions to the first two problems are in your hands. The third problem, that of negative attitudes, is probably the most difficult to solve. All you can do is to encourage appraisees to recognise for themselves that their attitudes are unhelpful. It is no good simply telling people that their attitudes are all wrong. You have to refer to specific instances where performance has not met expectations and try to help appraisees to understand that in these particular cases they would have got better results by, for example, being more cooperative. Asking fairly pointed questions might be necessary, for example:

O Do you think that you would have done better in this instance if you had taken more account of the other person's point of view?

○ Frankly, on this occasion you didn't seem too keen to get on with it. Could you tell me why?

○ You tell me that you're not getting the sort of cooperation you need from your colleagues. But this incident seems to indicate to me that you have not always cooperated well with them. Would you like to comment?

○ There have been a number of occasions during the last few months when you have given me the impression that you weren't at all happy about doing what you were asked to do. For example, there was the time I asked you to investigate that complaint from Brown Brothers, and the incident when I wanted you to carry out an urgent performance analysis of our Northern Region suppliers... Could you tell me why you reacted in this way?

Problems related to gaps in knowledge or skills or failure to meet acceptable levels of competence also may be hard to deal with, but at least you can adopt an analytical approach which avoids the emotional reactions which may result from a direct accusation that someone's attitudes are negative. It is generally better to concentrate on these factors affecting performance rather than plunge into the dangerous waters of attitude assessment.

This approach is eased if there are clearly defined and agreed specifications of knowledge and skill requirements and competence frameworks exist which have been derived from proper skills and competence analysis. These will provide criteria against which the attributes and job-related behaviour of appraisees can be measured and discussed. Approaches to analysing levels of competence are described below.

ANALYSE LEVELS OF COMPETENCE

Levels of competence are best measured by reference to a competence framework which describes what is required under various headings.

One approach, as adopted by the National Australian Group, is to define various performance criteria covering knowledge, skill and competence. Their ten performance guideline headings are as follows:

O *Professional and technical knowledge*. Command and use of relevant professional/technical and job related knowledge and skills.

O *Organisational and business knowledge*. Effective knowledge of the organisation and an appreciation of the wider business issues.

O *Interpersonal and communications*. Ability to relate to others both one to one and in teams, and to give and receive messages, face to face and in writing.

O *Influencing skills*. Taking action to affect the behaviour and decisions of other people.

O *Critical thinking*. Being able to make sense of issues, identify and solve problems and 'think on one's feet'.

O *Self-managing and learning*. Ability to maintain appropriately directed energy and stamina to exercise self-control and to learn new behaviours.

O *Achievement and action*. Focus on achieving results, keenness to 'get going and keep going'.

O *Initiative and innovation*. Creates and appreciates new ideas and perspectives. Sees possibilities and challenges established practices in constructive ways.

O *Strategic perspectives*. Being able to think broadly, analyse the 'big picture' and value diverse perspectives.

O *Capacity for change*. Ability to cope with continuous and complex changes, to be flexible and to handle high degrees of uncertainty.

In the guidelines for appraisees published by the National Australian Group it is stated that:

It is important that you agree what is expected of you for each of these performance criteria. To help you and your appraiser do this a set of performance guidelines has been produced. You should consider each of the ten performance criteria and plan where improvement is needed. Some criteria will be more important than others and it is on these that you and your appraiser should focus.

Separate performance guidelines are defined for clerical staff, supervisors, managers, senior managers and executive staff. The guidelines for managers read as follows:

Professional and technical knowledge

○ Has expertise in the productive marketing of the business unit's services.

○ Has expert knowledge of business unit's services and sufficient familiarity with other business units' services to enable customer needs to be met.

○ Has expert knowledge of basic operations of the total business unit and the appropriate management information.

Organisational and business knowledge

○ Understands and applies organisational knowledge to the business unit.

○ Knows who to contact to gain additional knowledge.

○ Appropriately applies knowledge of the team to enhance the operations of the business unit.

Interpersonal and communications

○ Responds constructively when dealing with customers and colleagues.

○ Can establish rapport easily with a range of different people.

○ Helps people in groups and teams to 'get on together'.

○ Can say 'no' when necessary and set standards/limits for others.

○ Makes it easy for others to be open and honest.

○ Presents ideas and information clearly in speech and writing.

Influencing skills

○ Maintains good relations with customers even when their needs can't all be met.

○ Actively involves others in decision making and wins cooperation.

○ Uses contacts appropriately to obtain information and help.

○ Is assertive for self and/or on team's behalf without damaging relationships.

Critical thinking

○ Readily spots trends and patterns in job-related quantitative and qualitative data.

○ Tests the quality of available information and draws logical conclusions from it.

○ Can analyse varied major problems and at the same time identify appropriate action.

Self-managing and learning

○ Is objective about own strengths and weaknesses.

○ Prepared to back own judgement publicly.

○ Keeps calm under pressure.

○ Concentrates and maintains focus, even when constantly interrupted.

○ Makes good use of opportunities to learn.

○ Recognises and deals effectively with personal stress.

Achievement and action

○ Is clear about what 'success' means for the business; successful in overcoming obstacles.

○ Makes decisions without 'passing the buck' and sets personal performance standards.

○ Takes early action to deal with problems even if it is difficult or unpopular.

○ Makes best use of resources to achieve objectives.

Initiative and innovation

- ○ Identifies options for improvement and acts on them – or motivates others to do so.
- ○ Challenges accepted ways of doing things, even when this means breaking with 'time honoured' traditions.
- ○ Actively encourages the team to come up with new ideas and approaches.
- ○ Experiments and learns from mistakes.

Strategic perspectives

- ○ Understands key organisational aims, values and strategies.
- ○ Anticipates how trends and events in different areas of the business and environment will affect them.
- ○ Actively encourages and supports people when they offer different perspectives and opinions.

Capacity for change

- ○ Gradually modifies approach or strategy as the situation changes.
- ○ Can accept and work with new approaches, even if not totally in agreement with them. Keeps focused in the face of uncertainty. Helps the team to accept and adjust to changed approaches.
- ○ Matches opinions in response to contrary evidence. Can modify own style when appropriate.

Performance in relation to guidelines is analysed jointly in the appraisal meeting. This means taking each guideline in turn, discussing what it means in relation to the appraisee's job, modifying it as necessary to suit any special requirements and, by reference to results and events agreeing on the level of competence the appraisee has attained. Comments are then agreed and a criteria assessment is made for each heading using the following scale:

1. Performance consistently exceeds all requirements associated with the job.

2. Performance consistently meets all requirements of the job, and regularly exceeds expectations.
3. Performance consistently meets all requirements of the job.
4. Performance meets most of the requirements but not all. Further improvement is required.
5. Performance does not meet the standards associated with the job.

An overall assessment of performance is also made using a similar rating scale.

This approach defines each requirement positively and leaves the appraiser and the appraisee to agree on the extent to which performance has fallen above or below the standard.

Some performance guideline approaches define both positive and negative indicators – using what are sometimes termed 'differentiating competences'. This is an example of the leadership competence dimension used by a large retail group:

Definition

Guiding, encouraging and motivating individuals and teams to achieve a desired result.

Positive indicators

○ Achieves high level of performance from team.
○ Defines objectives, plans and expectations clearly.
○ Continually monitors performance and provides good feedback.
○ Maintains effective relationships with individuals and the team as a whole.
○ Develops a sense of common purpose in the team.
○ Builds team morale and effectively motivates individual members of the team by recognising their contribution while taking appropriate action to deal with poor performers.

Negative indicators

○ Does not achieve high levels of performance from team.

○ Fails to clarify objectives or standards of performance.

○ Pays insufficient attention to the needs of individuals and the team.

○ Neither monitors nor provides effective feedback on performance.

○ Inconsistent in rewarding good performance or taking action to deal with poor performers.

The advantage of scales such as the two examples given above is that they do provide a framework for making assessments on the basis of agreed and understood definitions of the criteria which should be used. Appraisers are thus less likely to get into the difficulties they may meet if they try to tackle what they regard as poor attitudes. In fact, there is much to be said for relying on such guidelines entirely when assessing the reasons for achieving certain levels of performance on the grounds that they are, or at least should be, related to specific behaviours rather than abstract attitudes. And it can always be argued that an attitude is only relevant if it does affect the sort of behaviours that such competence frameworks define.

PROVIDE FEEDBACK

Although self-appraisal is a useful way of getting people to analyse their own performance there will still be many occasions during both formal and informal appraisal discussions and, indeed, during the normal course of day-to-day work when appraisers must provide some feedback to appraisees. Appraisers are, after all, usually in a better position to assess the contributions of individuals within the context of the efforts of the whole team or department.

In systems engineering, feedback transmits information on performance from one part of a system to an earlier part of the system in order to generate corrective action or to initiate new action.

In this respect at least, performance appraisal has some of the characteristics of a system in that it provides for information to be presented (feedback) to people on their performance, which helps them to understand how well they have been doing and how effective their behaviour has been. The aim is for feedback to promote this understanding so that appropriate action can be taken. This can be corrective action where the feedback has revealed that something has gone wrong or, more positively, action taken to make the best use of the opportunities the feedback has revealed.

Systems engineers design self-regulating systems which generate their own feedback and respond to this information of their own volition. The same principle can be applied in performance appraisal – individuals can be encouraged to understand the performance measures which are available for them to use in order to provide their own feedback and to develop their own plans for performance improvement and development.

Such self-generated feedback is a highly desirable feature of a full performance appraisal process but there will always be a need for managers, colleagues and, sometimes, internal or external advisers to provide feedback based on their own observations and understanding.

Feedback in performance appraisal is positive in the sense that its aim is to point the way to further development and improvement, not simply to tell people where they have gone wrong (negative feedback). But feedback must report on shortcomings as well as achievements, although if there have been any failings they should not be dwelt on as matters for blame. Instead, they should be treated as opportunities for learning so that they are less likely to be repeated in the future.

Feedback in performance appraisal is always factual. It refers to results, events, critical incidents and significant behaviours which have affected performance in specific ways. The feedback should be recognised and accepted by individuals as a matter of fact not of opinion. Of course there will often be room for some interpretation of the facts but such interpretations should start from the actual situation as reported in the feedback not from the subjective views expressed by the provider of the feedback.

Guidelines On Providing Feedback

○ *Build feedback into the job.* To be effective feedback should be built into the job or provided as quickly as possible after the activity taking place, ideally within a day or two.

○ *Provide feedback on actual events.* Feedback should be provided on actual results or observed behaviour. It should not be based on supposition about the reason for the behaviour. You should, for example, say: 'We have received a complaint from a customer that you have been rude, would you like to comment on this', rather than: 'You tend to be aggressive'.

○ *Describe, don't judge.* The feedback should be presented as a description of what has happened, it should not be accompanied by a judgement. If you start by saying: 'I have been informed that you have been rude to one of our customers; we can't tolerate that sort of behaviour' you will instantly create resistance and prejudice an opportunity to encourage improvement.

○ *Refer to specific behaviours.* Relate all your feedback to specific items of behaviour. Do not indulge in transmitting general feelings or impressions.

○ *Ask questions.* Ask questions rather than make statements: 'Why do you think this happened?'; 'On reflection is there any other way in which you think you could have handled the situation?'; 'How do you think you should tackle this sort of situation in the future?'

○ *Select key issues.* Select key issues and restrict yourself to them. There is a limit to how much criticism anyone can take. If you overdo it, the shutters will go up and you will get nowhere.

○ *Focus.* Focus on aspects of performance the individual can improve. It is a waste of time to concentrate on areas which the individual can do little or nothing about.

○ *Provide positive feedback.* Provide feedback on the things that the individual did well in addition to areas for improvement. People are more likely to work positively at improving their performance and developing their skills if they feel empowered by the process.

9

Interpersonal Skills

THE NATURE OF INTERPERSONAL SKILLS

Interpersonal or interactive skills are those used by people to build and maintain relationships with one another in order to achieve a purpose (which may or may not be articulated). The social interaction which takes place when using interpersonal skills involves both verbal behaviour (asking or replying to questions, making statements, negotiating etc), or non-verbal behaviour (facing people, looking at them, reacting physically to what they say or do etc by nodding, smiling etc).

Interpersonal skills are exercised when someone, for example an appraiser, initiates action to achieve an aim which is dependent on the reaction and agreement of another person – for example, an appraisee. The latter may have their own objectives and will certainly not be inert or passive. Appraisees will produce behaviours and reactions which have to be taken into account by appraisers, who will order their behaviour in a way it is believed will contribute to achieving their objectives. Appraisers have to ensure that appraisees will interact with them productively and this will be affected by how appraisers see appraisees and vice versa.

The attitudes of appraisers will depend partly on their knowledge of the appraisees, but may be affected by deeper rooted feelings about people in general or the appraisees in particular. These attitudes will affect the appraisers' behaviours towards the appraisees. One of the key attributes required to understand the behaviour of another person is empathy or social sensitivity. This involves the ability to put oneself in another's place by receiving and correctly interpreting a wide range of clues from them and assessing their feelings, attitudes and reactions carefully.

The interpersonal skills discussed in this chapter will be concerned with eliciting information about the other person by asking the right questions, listening carefully, being sensitive to the other person's concerns, observing and responding to non-verbal signals, maintaining open, friendly body language, being open to criticism, being assertive and reaching agreement.

ASKING THE RIGHT QUESTIONS

Effective interaction will be enhanced by asking the right sort of questions – those that elicit a positive response and encourage participation and a conversational flow during the discussion, thus contributing to mutual understanding and agreement on what the issues are and what needs to be done about them.

There are four basic types of questions:

Open Questions

Open questions are general, not specific. They provide room for appraisees to decide on how they should be answered and encourage them to talk freely. A relaxed and friendly start can be made to a meeting by the use of such questions. They can set the scene for the more detailed analysis of performance that will follow later and can be introduced at any point to open up a discussion on a new topic.

Open questions help to create an atmosphere of calm and friendly enquiry and can be expressed quite informally, for example:

○ How do you think things have been going?

○ What do you feel about that?

○ How can we build on that in the future?

○ What can we learn from that?

Open questions can be put in a 'tell me' form such as:

○ Tell me, why do you think that happened?

○ Tell me, how did you handle that situation?

○ Tell me, how is that project going?

○ Tell me, what are your key objectives going to be next year?

Probing Questions

Open questions will get appraisees to talk generally about their work but it will also be necessary to focus on particular issues from time to time – seeking information is one of the prime purposes of an appraisal discussion.

Probing questions ask for specific information on what has happened and why it has happened. They examine closely the steps that need to be taken to put things right, do better in the future and avoid repeating a mistake.

As suggested by Ian Mackay (*A Manager's Guide to the Appraisal Discussion*, BACIE, 1992), probe questions can be used in three ways:

1. *To show interest and encouragement* by making supportive statements followed by questions, for example: 'I see, and then what?'

2. *To seek further information* by:
   — simple interrogation, 'Why?' or 'Why not?'
   — extension, 'How do you mean?'

3. *To explore opinions and attitudes in detail* by:
   — opinion investigating, 'To what extent do you feel that...?'
   — reflection, 'Am I right in inferring from what you have just said that it seems to you that....?' or 'Have I got the right impression, do you feel that...?'

When using probe questions you should not be subjecting appraisees to an interrogation. You are not there to make appraisees 'see the error of their ways' and leave it at that. Your job is to encourage them to go into more detail about specific aspects of their performance, explaining in their own words the circumstances, the reasons and the implications for the future. This may well mean that they will be asked to reveal aspects of their performance which they would prefer not to discuss. Often there will be occasions when you have to get appraisees to face up to facts because if they do not recognise the need for improvement they will not agree to do anything about it.

When faced with the need to dig deeper you have to be careful not to frame your questions in a hostile way. Ask: 'Why, exactly, do you think that happened?' or 'Could you give me more details of the circumstances which created that situation?', rather than: 'Something went very wrong there, how could you have allowed that to happen?' or 'That was a bad mistake, what on earth persuaded you to make it?' Phrasing questions too negatively may produce equally negative or defensive reactions, and you would have to resort to telling the appraisee what you think, which is less likely to produce a positive result although you may sometimes have no alternative but to spell it out. It is worth repeating that appraisal is not just about being nice to people. You have sometimes 'to be cruel only to be kind'; in other words you have to ensure that appraisees know that they have not met agreed performance expectations and if you cannot encourage them to recognise this for themselves you have to point it out.

Probing questions can help to change negatives into positives. You could, for example, approach a failure to achieve an objective like this:

> What we've just been talking about shows that you didn't achieve your target, what exactly do you think must be done to get better results next year?

Or if a bad mistake has been repeated and cannot be recalled by the appraisee you could start with a reminder of the occasions, and then go on to probe into why this was happening and what could be done about it:

> You remember that in December last we talked about the situation which arose when you dealt with a similar enquiry and how you could avoid making the same mistake again. But as you will recall, you made a very similar error in February. We discussed the problem then, but I think we need to reflect now on what actions are required to be quite sure that it never happens again. So tell me

why you think these things are happening and what you think must be done to ensure that there won't be a recurrence.

Probing questions are designed to get to the heart of the matter but always with the aim of identifying future developmental or performance improvement needs. Their aim is to ensure that both parties 'know the reasons for things' so that action plans can be agreed.

This type of question need not always focus on what seems to have gone wrong. It can be phrased neutrally to establish just what is happening and why. For example:

○ Tell me, exactly what happened there?

○ How do you explain the outcome of your project?

○ What are the factors that have contributed to that result?

If a satisfactory result has been achieved, appraisees can be encouraged to carry on as before, or possibly more so if you would like an even better result. Alternatively, if it is established that things have gone wrong and that there is room for improvement, remedial action should be discussed and this should be prompted by specific and quite tough questions such as:

○ What do you think needs to be done to improve your ability to cope with this sort of situation?

○ What steps are you going to take to ensure that you fully understand this procedure in future?

○ How can we ensure that this does not happen again?

○ What do you think you need to do to avoid making the same mistake?

Closed Questions

Open and probing questions invite appraisees to expand and talk freely and are therefore the most useful way of ensuring that the discussion does indeed become 'a conversation with a purpose'. However, you may need to obtain or confirm specific factual data, and in that case you can ask a closed question which severely restricts the reply to supplying the information required. For example:

O How many times has this happened?

O When did this take place?

O Who else was involved?

O How long have you spent on this project?

O Is it the case that...?

Closed questions are easy to answer and are often necessary to elicit the facts. However, they should be used with discretion because they can degenerate into an interrogation and this will inhibit the free flow of information and comment which is an essential part of a productive appraisal discussion.

Leading Questions

Leading questions are those which supply their own 'right' answer, for example:

O Do you agree that...?

O Can you deny that...?

O Wouldn't you say that...?

O Isn't it the case that...?

If you ask questions like these you are simply saying 'tell me what I want to hear' and that will get you nowhere.

Overall Approach to Asking Questions

A typical appraisal discussion contains a mix of open, probing and closed questions. Get and keep the conversation going with open questions, ensure that you identify the real issues with probing questions and get the facts with closed questions, but use the latter with care. Do not ask leading questions.

Ian Wright's (ibid) prescriptions for effective questions are:

O Keep the purpose of the appraisal discussion clearly in mind.

O Use plain language.

○ Allow thinking time for response.

○ Maintain an atmosphere of friendly neutrality.

○ Do not talk too much.

Additional ways of improving effectiveness are:

○ Ask one question at a time – if you pile too many on top of one another the appraisee will be confused and may duck those they do not want to answer.

○ Check and, if necessary, play back the points appraisees are making if they are unclear or seemingly irrational – do this neutrally and appraisees may appreciate that they have not expressed themselves well or are being irrational – throughout the discussion you should take whatever steps are necessary to test your understanding.

LISTEN CAREFULLY

An appraisal discussion is a dialogue: both parties are communicating information and ideas to one another to achieve the purpose of the meeting. A dialogue will involve asking and replying to questions but it will get nowhere if neither party really listens to what the other is saying.

There is an old adage: 'Hearing is with the ears, listening is with the mind'. It is not enough just to hear what someone else says. You listen with your mind as well. There are many good writers and speakers but few good listeners. Most of us filter the spoken words addressed to us so that we absorb only some of them – frequently those we want to hear. Listening is an art which not many people cultivate. But it is a very necessary one, because a good listener will gather more information and achieve better rapport with the other person. Both these effects of good listening are essential to good communications, and good communications are the essence of an effective appraisal discussion.

People do not listen because they are:

○ unable to concentrate, for whatever reason;

O too pre-occupied with themselves;

O over-concerned with what they are going to say next;

O uncertain about what they are listening to or why they are listening to it;

O unable to follow the points or arguments made by the speaker;

O simply not interested in what is being said.

Good listeners:

O concentrate on the speaker, following not only words but also body language which, through the use of eyes or gestures, often underlines meaning and gives life to the message;

O respond quickly to points made by the speaker, if only in the shape of encouraging grunts;

O ask questions frequently to elucidate meaning and to give the speaker an opportunity to rephrase or underline a point;

O comment on the points made by the speaker, without interrupting the flow, in order to test understanding and demonstrate that the speaker and listener are still on the same wavelength. These comments may reflect back or summarise something the speaker has said, thus giving an opportunity for him or her to reconsider or elucidate the point made;

O make notes on the key points – even if the notes are not referred to later they will help to concentrate the mind;

O are continuously evaluating the messages being delivered to check that they are understood and relevant to the purpose of the meeting;

O are alert at all times to the nuances of what the speaker is saying;

O are prepared to let the speaker go on with the minimum of interruption;

O are patient – they give speakers time to think and to articulate their thoughts.

BODY LANGUAGE

Words are not the only means of communication. The ways in which you present yourself and react physically can convey very clearly the extent to which you are really listening to what people have to say. This is sometimes called physical attending and involves:

○ facing other people squarely so that you are seen to be listening and responding to what they have to say;

○ maintaining good eye contact to demonstrate that you are attending – look the other person in the eye rather than somewhere over his or her shoulder, without, of course, subjecting them to an unrelenting stare;

○ maintaining an open posture to demonstrate that you are receptive to their ideas or comments – do not create barriers by hunching over papers behind your desk ;

○ showing that you are interested by leaning slightly forward rather than lolling about and giving the impression that you are bored with the whole affair;

○ smiling encouragingly from time to time – but do not allow a senseless grin to remain on your face;

○ nodding in agreement when you want to signal that you are getting the message and are happy with it – you can reinforce your affirmatory nods with encouraging grunts or other oral interjections such as 'good', 'I see', 'well, that makes sense';

○ but do not overdo this sort of language, only use it when you feel that it will help to make appraisees believe that you are attending to what they say and approve it;

○ conversely, however, do not shake your head or grimace if appraisees say something with which you disagree – in this situation your approach should be to remain neutral and use oral means to convey that you have a different point of view;

○ remaining relaxed, as if you are tense this will be communicated to the appraisee who may become equally tense, thus eliminating any hope of a productive dialogue – an attitude of physical composure will encourage an open and responsive relationship.

OBSERVING BODY LANGUAGE

Just as you can communicate through your own body language you can help in the process of 'getting the message' by observing the body language of appraisees. Facial expressions and physical gestures will give some indication of the degree to which appraisees are taking an active interest in the discussion, listening to your questions or comments, agreeing or disagreeing with what you say, or are apprehensive, angry (for whatever reason), bored or indifferent.

SENSITIVITY TO THE APPRAISEE'S CONCERNS

Appraisers are more likely to guide the discussion to a successful conclusion if they are sensitive to the appraisees' concerns. This involves empathy – putting yourself in the other person's place and trying to understand their point of view. This does not mean that understanding will inevitably bring agreement. You may establish that there are significant differences between your stance and that of appraisees. At least this identifies areas where you may have to strive harder for agreement and may show the way to the line you should take in persuading appraisees to look at things from a different viewpoint.

BEING RESPONSIVE TO CRITICISM

You should give appraisees the opportunity to comment on how they feel about your actions as a manager or team leader in such areas as clarifying expectations, giving them adequate (but not oppressive) attention, delegating work, providing feedback and guiding or helping them as required. You can get enlightening comments in response to such questions as:

○ Is there anything about the way I am doing my job which makes your job more difficult?

○ Is there anything I could do which would make it easier to achieve your targets?

○ Are you satisfied that you have the opportunity to make good use of your knowledge and skills?

If comments from appraisees contain criticisms you have to be able to handle them without getting angry or defensive. There are a number of possible reactions to criticism:

○ You may be able to refute criticism by bringing factual evidence to bear which confounds it. But this should be done calmly and coolly. You can be assertive in maintaining your point of view, as discussed in the next section of this chapter, but you should not be aggressive.

○ You may have to accept some criticism by acknowledging that there is some truth in it, but you might still want to reserve the right to be the best judge of what you do.

○ You may accept that the criticism is valid, but there is no need to apologise as long as you initiate a discussion about how to improve things.

ON BEING ASSERTIVE

An appraisal discussion will lose effectiveness if either party is too submissive – allowing themselves to be unduly influenced by the other's point of view, especially when it is expressed forcibly. Assertive people are those who stand up for their own rights in ways which do not violate other people's rights. They express their opinions, feelings, beliefs and needs in honest and appropriate terms. Being assertive is not the same as being aggressive, which means violating other people's rights in order to get your own way.

In an appraisal discussion, assertive behaviour by either party puts them into the position of being able to influence the other party properly and to react to them positively. Assertive statements:

○ are brief and to the point;
○ indicate clearly that you are not hiding behind something and are speaking for yourself by using words such as 'I feel that...',

'I believe that...', 'I think that...' – your beliefs and views are important;

○ are not overweighted with advice;

○ use questions to find out the views of others and to test their reactions to your behaviour;

○ distinguish between fact and opinion;

○ are expressed positively but not dogmatically;

○ indicate that you are aware that the other person may have a different point of view;

○ express, where necessary, negative feelings about the effects of other people's behaviour on you – pointing out in dispassionate and factual terms the feelings aroused in you by the behaviour, and suggesting the behaviour you would prefer;

○ point out to the other person politely but firmly the consequences of their behaviour.

There may be situations where you want to make a point but the other person does not want to cooperate. When this happens you can patiently and calmly repeat your words until the person recognises your insistence and appreciates that you are not going to let the topic drop. This example of a conversation illustrates how such a discussion might proceed:

'Let's talk about how we can improve the way in which we handle customer queries'.

'But that's nothing to do with me, queries are dealt with in customer relations'.

'Yes, I appreciate that, but your job is concerned generally with market development and wouldn't you agree that the way we handle our customers is relevant?'

'Yes, but I have a lot of other things on my plate and, frankly, I haven't the time to be bothered about the routines of dealing with queries.'

'OK, I understand, but I would still value your views.'

'But it's your problem not mine.'

'Yes, I accept that it may look like that from your point of view but I really would like to discuss it from your perspective'.

In this example the appraiser has acknowledged the other person's point of view but has persisted in indicating that the appraisee's own ideas are wanted without being aggressive and thereby creating a negative reaction.

REACHING AGREEMENT

Agreement on a performance issue or an improvement plan is most likely to be achieved if you recognise the other person's concerns and feelings, obtain and listen carefully to their views and adopt a joint problem-analysis and problem-solving approach.

You may, however, have to use influencing skills to obtain agreement. The four influencing styles you can use are:

1. *Asserting* – making your views clear.
2. *Persuading* – using facts, logic and reason to present your case, emphasising its strong points, anticipating objections, appealing to reason, and demonstrating how the other person will benefit.
3. *Bridging* – drawing out the other person's point of view, demonstrate that you appreciate their concerns and understand what they are getting at, giving credit and praise in response to their good ideas, joining your views with theirs.
4. *Attracting* – conveying your enthusiasm for their ideas, getting people to feel that they are part of an attractive project.

BENEFITS FROM USING INTERPERSONAL SKILLS EFFECTIVELY

The benefits from the effective use of interpersonal skills in an appraisal discussion are as follows:

O A two-way dialogue is maintained which ensures the active participation of appraisees and reduces defensiveness, builds commitment, makes the appraiser more of a coach and less of a judge, and encourages the appraisee to produce ideas.

O The real issues concerning performance and development are thoroughly addressed and understood.

O Appraisers obtain insight into the views and attitudes of appraisees and their reasons for behaving in particular ways.

O Appraisees feel valued at the end of the discussion because appraisers listen to them, demonstrate that they understand the appraisees' problems and comment fairly on their performance.

O Appraisees learn how to make even better use of their strengths and what action they need to take to overcome any shortcomings.

O Appraisers learn what they need to do to help appraisees improve their performance and, incidentally but importantly, learn about their effectiveness as leaders.

O The accountabilities of appraisees for achieving results and the expectations of appraisees about the standards of performance required are clarified.

O Agreement is reached at the end of the discussion on what both parties should do in the future.

These are exacting requirements and they make considerable demands on the skills both parties have to use on a person-to-person basis to build and maintain good and productive relationships. This is why both appraisers and appraisees require training in the use of these skills. Too often appraisal training is directed at appraisers and the needs of appraisees are neglected. It is no wonder that in these circumstances appraisees may feel that appraisal is something which is being done to them rather than a process in which they take an active part.

10
Completing the discussion

STEPS TO BE TAKEN

The main steps to be taken when completing the discussion are to:

○ check understanding;
○ plan ahead;
○ rate performance, if that is part of the process;
○ complete documentation;
○ end the meeting on a positive note.

Check Understanding

When the discussion has been completed it is essential to check with appraisees their understanding of what has been said and agreed. If necessary, time must be spent in clarifying that under-standing. There should be no doubts in the minds of either party about the conclusions reached. It is to be hoped that complete accord will have been achieved but if a disagreement has not been resolved during the discussion, then there must be 'an agreement to differ' which can be recorded. In those circum-stances, it is most important to make plans to deal with the prob-lem in a further meeting, which should not be unduly delayed. A review by the appraiser's manager may also contribute to the resolution of disagreements.

Plan Ahead

The importance of completing the discussion with such a review cannot be underestimated. Appraisal discussions are held for one reason only: to prepare and agree plans for the future on the basis of an analysis of past performance and anticipated requirements. In performance management systems this plan is often called a performance agreement or contract and this terminology applies equally to performance appraisal. In fact, the approach to performance appraisal described in this book has most, if not all, the characteristics of a fully developed performance management system.

The term performance planning is sometimes used to describe the whole process of forming an agreement and then expressing it as a number of actions to be taken by the individual, by the manager or by the individual and the manager jointly.

Rate Performance

Many, although not all, performance appraisal schemes include a performance rating section in which an assessment of performance is made by the manager under a number of different headings and/or overall. Such a rating system is often associated with a performance-related pay scheme, although there are strong arguments for carrying out ratings for performance pay purposes on a separate occasion.

Documentation

Once the performance agreement has been completed, it can be documented and, if this is felt to be appropriate, reviewed by the appraiser's manager, sometimes called, rather patronisingly, a 'grandparent' review.

Final Points

The following checklist summarises the key points to which you should give attention at the end of the meeting:

1. Summarise action points and end on a positive note.
2. Agree and record the key points of the discussion.
3. Ensure you complete the actions to which you have agreed.
4. Agree appropriate time-scales for reviews.

5. Set up arrangements for monitoring progress against objectives so that you can be alerted to any potential problems.

Plan of This Chapter

This chapter examines the processes involved in:

○ completing performance agreements;

○ rating performance;

○ documenting the results of the discussion and the performance agreement;

○ using a performance-related training approach to ensure that development and improvement plans are implemented.

COMPLETING PERFORMANCE AGREEMENTS

Performance agreements and plans set the direction and form the basis for measurement, feedback, assessment and development in the performance appraisal process. They are sometimes referred to as performance contracts or, to emphasise the developmental nature of appraisal, performance and development agreements.

A performance agreement defines expectations – the work to be done, the results to be attained and the attributes (skills, knowledge and expertise) and competences required to achieve these results. It also identifies the measures used to monitor, review and assess performance and sets out agreed plans for the next period for development and performance improvement.

Performance agreements and plans are normal processes of management, not just components in a performance appraisal 'system'. While it may be necessary to talk about 'performance appraisal' to get the concept across to everyone and to provide a basis for developing the skills required, this should not be overdone.

If too much is made of the content and the special 'processes' involved in performance appraisal there is a danger of managers regarding it as something they do because they are told to do it – an add-on activity to their real job. But there is much to be said for providing a framework to guide managers on how this important part of their job should be carried out and this is what a performance agreement does.

A typical performance agreement will incorporate:

○ any changes or additions to job requirements which need to be incorporated in a revised job description;

○ revised or new objectives;

○ reference to any work plans required to meet job requirements and objectives;

○ a performance improvement and development plan.

Job Requirements

It is essential at the end of the discussion to review any changes or additions that have been or are about to be made to job requirements. These could include increased responsibility, extra tasks, additional resources to be controlled or any other new features of the job. They should be incorporated as amendments to the job description. In this way the description is regularly updated and can form a satisfactory base for setting objectives and monitoring performance. Too often, job descriptions are allowed to get out of date and this will prejudice the results obtained from the performance appraisal discussion, which must always be rooted in what the appraisee is actually doing rather than some theoretical role definition. This revised description is then used as the framework for the review of objectives and plans.

Objectives

To update objectives it is necessary to examine each of the tasks set out in the revised job description and establish whether or not there is any need to change any of the standing or continuing objectives related to particular tasks. This may involve re-examining existing standards of performance to ensure that they are still appropriate.

It is then necessary to look at any specific and quantifiable targets which should be attached to specified areas of activities. Starting from those that have been set previously, as described in Chapter 4, any changes required can be discussed and agreed. These changes may reflect new targets for the organisation, department or team which have to be reflected in individual target levels.

This should not, however, be regarded as solely a top-down process. Although there will be overriding organisational and departmental targets which have to be achieved as far as is humanly possible, appraisees should be given the opportunity to comment on these requirements as they affect them and make suggestions as to how their own targets should fit those determined for a higher level. They must also be allowed to comment on the reasonableness of the targets. If they feel that they cannot be attained, they should be able to say so. They may have a good point to make which should be taken into account. Even if their reservations are difficult to accept because they prejudice the ability of appraisers to reach their targets, at least appraisers will know in good time of a potential problem and be able to do something about it, possibly by reassigning work or providing extra help, guidance or training.

Any new objectives agreed should meet the criteria set out in Chapter 4 (page 43), ie they should be 'SMART'.

Discussions on the objectives to be attained also should refer to any corporate values in such areas as quality, teamwork and innovation, and what appraisees are expected to do to ensure that they are upheld.

Work plans

Work planning is the normal activity of preparing and agreeing programmes for the achievement of objectives. It is a continuing activity because of the need to revise and update work plans to meet new demands or situations.

Work plans set out how objectives are to be attained. They define programmes of work for achieving targets, improving performance or completing projects. They also establish priorities – the key aspects of the job to which attention has to be given, or the order of importance of the various projects or programmes of work the individual is expected to undertake. The aim is to ensure that the meaning of the objectives and performance standards as they apply to everyday work is understood. They are the basis for converting aims into action.

Performance Improvement and Development Plans

The performance and development plan incorporated in the performance agreement records the actions agreed to improve performance and to develop attributes and competences. The performance plan is likely to concentrate on development in the current job – to improve the ability to perform it well and also, importantly, to enable individuals to take on wider responsibilities, extending their capacity to undertake a broader role. This plan therefore contributes to the achievement of a policy of continuous development which is predicated on the belief that everyone is capable of learning more and doing better in their jobs. But the plan will also contribute to enhancing the potential of individuals to carry out higher level jobs.

The performance and development plan must clearly be based on the outcome of the appraisal discussion. This will note any areas where the analysis has revealed that appraisees have not achieved a satisfactory level of competence in any aspect of their job or do not have the levels of attributes (knowledge, skills or expertise) required to carry out their job properly. This may be done by reference to a competence framework and to agreed specifications of the attributes required to achieve an acceptable level of performance as described in Chapter 4.

The plan should provide answers to the following questions which can be discussed with job holders:

O What areas of your performance do you feel in need of development?

○ What do you think you need to do to develop your performance in any particular areas?

○ Do you think you need further training in any aspect of your work?

○ How can I (ie the appraiser) help to improve your performance?

○ What development and training actions should we agree? (On the basis of the answers to the earlier questions.)

Performance improvement and development plans need to be devised and implemented in accordance with the principles of performance-related training as described in the last section of this chapter.

It is helpful to record agreements and plans for reference during the year (these should be working documents) and as a basis for progress reviews and revision in the light of changing circumstances. The performance agreement should not be recorded, as it were, on tablets of stone. It will almost inevitably have to be updated during the year if it is to retain its value as a basis for setting the direction, measuring progress and establishing priorities. Documentation and forms for this purpose are described later in this chapter and an example is given in Appendix B.

RATING

A method commonly used to summarise the judgements of appraisers is to get them to rate the performance of individuals on some form of scale. The rating scale format can be either behavioural, with examples of good, average and inadequate performance, or graphic which simply presents a number of scale points along a continuum. The scale points or anchors in the latter may be defined alphabetically (a,b,c etc), numerically (1,2,3 etc) or by means of initials (ex for excellent etc) which purport to disguise the hierarchical nature of the scale. The scale points may be further described adjectivally, for example: excellent (A), highly acceptable (B), acceptable (C), not entirely acceptable (D) and unacceptable (E).

The ratings might be made against a series of standard headings, which in traditional schemes were generalised performance characteristics or personality traits such as effective output, knowledge of work, judgement, initiative, cooperation and reliability.

In results-oriented schemes (ie those reviewing performance against objectives) a rating or indication of the level of achievement might be made of the level of achievement for each objective, for example: achieved, partly achieved, not achieved. Alternatively, or additionally, an overall rating of performance may be made using an alphabetical behaviourally defined scale.

Arguments For and Against Rating

The arguments for ratings are that:

○ they are a convenient way of summing up judgements which might otherwise be submerged in verbiage;

○ it is not possible to have performance-related pay without them (assuming that performance-related pay is wanted or needed);

○ they provide a means of identifying the exceptional performers or under-performers and those who are the reliable core performers so that action can be taken (developmental or some form of non-financial reward);

○ they can provide a basis for predicting potential on the assumption that people who perform well in the present are likely to go on doing so in the future – however, past performance is only a predictor of future performance when there is a connecting link, ie there are elements of the present job which are also important in a higher level job.

The arguments against ratings are that:

○ they are largely subjective and it is difficult to achieve consistency between different rates;

○ to sum up the total performance of a person with a single rating is a gross over-simplification of what may be a complex set of factors influencing that performance;

○ to make judgements about potential on the basis of an overall rating which masks dissimilarities between these elements is dangerous, although, obviously, poor overall performance should not be followed or rewarded by promotion;

○ to label people as 'average' or 'below average', or whatever equivalent terms are used, is both demeaning and demotivating.

Some organisations which do not have performance-related pay reject ratings altogether because of the objections listed above.

Organisations which do have performance-related pay may sometimes also avoid the use of performance ratings as part of the review system, and instead have a separate pay review in which managers are given a budget and simply asked to indicate whether they want to award an exceptionally high increase, an above average increase, a below average increase or no increase at all. Of course such judgements are related to assessments of performance and there is therefore a 'read across' from the review. But decisions about pay increases can be based on a number of factors besides performance in the current job, including the market worth of individuals and their potential.

Behaviourally Anchored Rating Scales

One of the approaches used by some organisations to overcome some of these problems mentioned is to use what are described as behaviourally anchored rating scales (BARS). These are designed to reduce the rating errors which it was assumed are typical of graphic scales. It is believed that the behavioural descriptions in such scales discourage the tendency to rate on the basis of generalised assumptions about personality traits (which were probably highly subjective) by focusing attention on specific work behaviours. An example is given in Chapter 4 (page 57):

Such scales are drawn up on the basis of research into what is regarded as the varying degrees of acceptability in behaviour with regard to an important performance dimension. They can help in making more objective judgements, but they are only really effective if they have been thoroughly researched and appraisers are well-trained in their use.

Considerations Affecting the Design and Use of Rating Scales

If ratings are to be included in a performance appraisal procedure three things need to be decided:

1. The basis on which levels of performance will be defined.
2. The number of rating levels to be used.
3. Methods of achieving a reasonable degree of accuracy and consistency in ratings.

These considerations are discussed in Chapter 14 (pages 173 to 184).

DOCUMENTATION

It has often been said in this book – but it bears repetition – that it is the processes of performance appraisal as practised by appraisers and appraisees which are important, not the content of the system; and the content often seems to consist largely of documents. Performance appraisal is about managing and improving performance. It is not about completing forms. The elegance with which forms are filled in is not important. Their purpose is no more than that of recording views and decisions; they are not ends in themselves, although this does not mean that if you do have appraisal forms, they should not be designed with care and produced to a reasonably high standard.

Many traditional merit rating or performance appraisal schemes appeared to be no more than form-filling exercises. Personnel managers spent their time chasing up reluctant line managers to complete their appraisal forms and return them to the personnel department, thus often unwittingly defeating the whole purpose of the exercise. Managers tended to be cynical about their rating and box-ticking activities and often produced bland and unrevealing reports which could be prepared without too much effort. They became even more cynical if they had any reason to believe that the completed forms were gathering dust in personal dossiers, unused and unheeded. Sadly, this was often what happened.

A case could be made for having no forms at all. Appraisers and appraisees could be encouraged to record the conclusions of their discussion and their agreements on blank sheets of paper to be used as working documents during the continuing process of managing performance throughout the year.

But there is much to be said for having a format which can help in the ordering and presentation of plans and comments. The mere existence of a form or a set of forms does demonstrate that this is a process which appraisers and appraisees are expected to take seriously.

Purpose

Before designing performance appraisal forms it is necessary to be quite clear about their purpose. The following questions need to be answered:

1. To what extent are these working documents for use by appraisers and appraisees?
2. What information does the human resources department need about the outcome of performance discussions?
3. How is the quality of performance discussions to be assured?
4. How can employees be reassured that they will not become the victims of prejudiced or biased reports?

Performance Appraisal Forms As Working Documents

The main function of performance appraisal forms is to act as working documents. They should be completed jointly by appraisers and appraisees. The appraiser should not deliver a filled-in form to an appraisee and say, 'What do you think?' In the past merit ratings were sometimes not shown to appraisees at all, which was a remarkable denial of the whole reason for appraisal.

Forms should be in continual use by appraisers and appraisees as reference documents on objectives and plans when reviewing progress. They should also record agreements on performance achievements and actions to be taken to improve performance or develop competence and skills. They should be dog-eared from much use – they should not be condemned to moulder away in a file.

It can be argued that for this reason the forms should be owned by the appraiser and the appraisee (both parties should have a copy). Any information the HR department needs in ratings (for performance-related pay or career planning purposes) or requests for training would be incorporated in a separate form for their use.

The appraisee can be protected against unfair assessments and ratings by providing for the appraiser's manager (the so-called 'grandparent') to see and comment on the completed report. These comments could be shown to appraisees who should have the right to appeal through a grievance procedure if they are still unhappy about the report.

There is, however, a good case for the human resources department having sight of completed review forms for quality assurance purposes, especially in the earlier days of operating performance management.

A typical set of forms which include an overall performance rating section is illustrated in Appendix B.

PERFORMANCE-RELATED TRAINING

Performance-related training needs are always defined and agreed specifically in terms of outcomes to be achieved by the individual with the help provided by the appraiser and other people. Definitions could be phrased like this:

○ At the end of this training or development programme I will be able to do x, y or z to an acceptable standard.

○ At the end of this training or development period I will be equipped to improve my performance in areas a, b or c, in these respects and to this extent.

The outcomes of performance-related training should always be measurable so that its effectiveness can be evaluated. A measurable outcome will be a specified increase in skill or gain in competence, or an observable and significant change in behaviour, or the achievement of higher levels of performance as indicated by attaining or surpassing quantified objectives in terms of targets, levels of service delivery etc.

Performance-related training needs are best met by on-the-job training and development, with the individuals being given the maximum encouragement, help and guidance to 'learn by doing'. A 'do-it-yourself' approach as described below is a good way of helping people to manage their own learning. This can be assisted by the provision of training modules, distance learning packs and guided reading lists produced by training specialists. The manager or team leader, however, still has a key role as a coach (see Chapter 13) and as a mentor (as discussed later in this chapter).

Self-Managed Learning

Self-managed learning starts with a definition of what someone needs to know or to do to be able to perform more effectively or to learn a skill. This should be established in the course of conducting performance reviews.

The next steps are to:

○ establish where the information needed to add knowledge or develop skills can be obtained – this may involve seeking help from a specialist trainer or making use of training and procedure manuals, computer-based training programmes, interactive video or guided reading lists;

○ give individuals an outline of the information they should obtain for themselves and where they can get it – they may be given questions to answer or mini-projects to complete;

○ decide what guidance or advice should be given to the individual and how it should be provided;

○ brief colleagues, people from other departments and specialist trainers/counsellors on the help they can provide;

○ prepare a timetable for the learning programme;

○ monitor the individual's progress, this should include periodical meetings to check on what has been learned and to provide more encouragement and guidance.

The Manager As Mentor

A mentor can be defined as an experienced and trusted adviser, and this is exactly what a good manager should be. Mentors play four roles: coach, teacher, sponsor and devil's advocate.

1. *Coach* – the mentor as coach encourages and stimulates people to decide what they need to learn and do to improve performance and prepare themselves for greater responsibilities. A coach points out the way and advises people how to make the best use of the learning opportunities provided by their job.

2. *Teacher* – the mentor as teacher may provide direct guidance on how the individual's work problems might be solved. In providing the guidance, however, a good mentor will ensure that learning takes place – in other words, individuals will know how to tackle the problem themselves next time. Managers acting as mentors can also teach skills more directly by holding 'What if...?' sessions in which they present problems to the individual or a group of individuals in the form of 'what if this situation arises – how would you deal with it?'

3. *Sponsor* – managers as mentors can create opportunities for individuals to prove themselves – to demonstrate what they have to offer. This can be done by setting 'stretch' targets, by

adding new challenges to the work role and by getting individuals to take part in project teams which will enlarge their understanding and skills.

4. *Devil's advocate* – managers can sometimes play the role of devil's advocate with individuals. They can challenge their assumptions and confront them with unusual ways of looking at things. They aim to give people practice in marshalling and presenting arguments, handling counter-arguments, and persuading others to accept their views. Managers can provide instances from their own experience of what works and what does not and can help to increase the individual's confidence in dealing with higher management or sceptical colleagues.

The associated role of coach and mentor is quite a demanding one and a few managers will not be up to it. They will need to be encouraged, persuaded and trained to carry it out. A good way of ensuring that they are fully aware of, and carry out, their responsibilities for developing their staff, is to include this as a key criterion in assessing their performance.

11

Performance Appraisal: Problems and Solutions

However worthwhile performance appraisal may be, it can be very difficult to get right. Numerous schemes have been started with a flourish of trumpets only to crash to the ground through the indifference or downright hostility of all concerned, except the personnel department.

What goes wrong can be one or more of the following:

○ attitudes;

○ support;

○ problems in making judgements about people;

○ lack of skill in conducting performance appraisal discussions;

○ difficulties in identifying the criteria for evaluating performance manifested in an inability to set good objectives or to find and use effective performance measures.

These problems and what can be done about them are discussed in this chapter.

NEGATIVE ATTITUDES TO PERFORMANCE APPRAISAL

There are many who believe in performance appraisal as a worthwhile method of analysing what people have done and are doing in a job to help them do it better. But there is a large population of managers and the managed who are hostile or indifferent to the process and/or do it badly if they do it at all.

Hostility From Managers

Hostility or indifference from managers arises because they believe that it is a waste of time. A typical reaction to the personnel department's proposal to introduce a new performance appraisal scheme is: 'Not another scheme, the last three didn't work!' Managers often claim that they are making judgements about their staff all the time – why go through this artificial and, to some, painful procedure of summing up in a few platitudinous phrases how their people are doing? They already know this perfectly well. The answer to this point is that they may feel they know, but they probably do not. All they obtain is a series of random impressions which may be culled from one or two recent incidents. Thus they ignore the longer term evidence which could be derived from a more systematic analysis of performance over the year and make partial, subjective and superficial judgements.

They may also feel that the scheme has nothing to do with their own needs and only exists to feed the personnel database. Too often the personnel department has contributed to this belief by adopting a 'policing' approach to the system, concerning themselves more with collecting completed forms and checking that each box has been ticked properly than with helping managers to use the process to improve individual, team and organisational performance, which is the only valid reason for its existence.

In short, managers tend to resist exhortations to conduct appraisal discussions conscientiously if at all because of:

○ mistrust of the usefulness and validity of the scheme itself;

○ a perceived lack of skill in handling appraisal discussions;

○ a dislike of criticising people to their face – many appraisers avoid this part of the discussion which thereby can lose much of its value;

○ a dislike of any new procedure imposed on them by others (eg the personnel department) which they see as interfering with their managerial prerogative of getting on with the job in their own way.

Attitudes like these can only be dispelled by ensuring that performance appraisal is fully owned and driven by line management. They must be involved in the development of the scheme and educated thoroughly on its purpose as an aid to the achievement of higher levels of performance for themselves by getting higher levels of performance from their staff. The personnel department has a part to play in developing performance appraisal and in monitoring its introduction and use. But their role is not to police the scheme. Instead, they are there to act as internal consultants and coaches, providing encouragement and guidance as required. It is certainly not their function to overburden managers with paperwork.

Hostility From Staff

Hostility among people at the receiving end can arise because, in spite of all the protestations of management to the contrary, they see performance appraisal as simply another weapon in the hands of managers to exercise their command and control prerogatives and to mobilise evidence which can be taken down and used against their subordinates. Even if they do not fear performance appraisal they observe managers going through the motions at performance review meetings – ticking boxes – and feel that the whole thing is just a rigmarole.

The initial response to these attitudes is education and training of both appraisers and appraisees on why the scheme exists, how it will operate to their mutual advantage and the part they will both play in ensuring its success. Involvement in developing the scheme is important and too much reliance should not be placed on leaflets and brochures – however glossy – or even videos to get the message across. Ultimately, 'the proof of the pudding will be in the eating', and fears will only be dispelled if the actual discussions do prove to be non-threatening and helpful.

SUPPORT

Top management may agree that there should be performance appraisal. The chief executive may write, or at least sign, the introduction to the handbook, or appear to say a few well chosen words at the beginning of the video. But this will be to no avail if thereafter they ignore the scheme or are seen to be paying only lip service to it. The success of performance appraisal depends on the continued support, encouragement and participation of senior management.

MAKING JUDGEMENTS ABOUT PEOPLE

Although the role of the appraiser is to be a helper rather than a judge, appraisal on a day-to-day basis as well as at more formal discussions will inevitably involve making judgements about people which will be recorded as comments or some form of rating. Most managers think they are good judges of people. Some no doubt are – they would not have got where they are if they were not. Others are not and you seldom if ever meet anyone who admits to this, just as one seldom hears anyone confessing that they are bad drivers – although accident rates suggest that bad drivers do exist – and mistakes in selection, placement and promotion indicate that some managers are worse than others in judging people.

Good judgement is a matter of having clearly defined standards available, considering only relevant evidence, avoiding projection (ascribing to other persons one's own unacceptable wants and faults) and combining probabilities in their correct weight.

The factors affecting assessments are those arising from:

O the characteristics of appraisers, including their ability to judge people and their attitudes to the process of assessment;

O the interaction between the appraiser and the appraisee;

O the way in which the appraisee is regarded by the appraiser which may mean stereotyping.

Characteristics of the Appraiser

Differences in personality characteristics will affect the type of judgements made and also the consistency and fairness of the judgements. As a result, the attitudes of appraisers to appraisees will vary and different appraisers may vary widely in their assessment of the same appraisee. One appraiser may rate everyone very generously (the all my geese are swans effect) while others may be exceptionally strict (all my swans are geese). Such differences in the levels of judgements and ratings arise where appraisers lack common standards by which to judge.

It has been discovered through research that if two appraisers rate the same appraisees, not only do they tend to rate at different standards but the spread or scatter of their ratings will vary. One appraisee, for example, will produce ratings that group fairly closely around the mean while the ratings of another appraiser will be much more widely scattered. It has been found that people who make snap judgements or jump to conclusions quickly tend to produce a wider scatter of judgements than those who are more deliberate and painstaking. It has also been found that people who produce a wide scatter of judgements tend to see things in extremes – as black or white rather than in shades of grey. The well known 'halo effect' or the lesser known 'horns effect' are associated with the spread factor. These effects arise when the appraiser focuses on some prominent or recent example of good or bad performance and assumes from this that all aspects of the job holder's performance are equally good or bad. This tendency to be over-influenced by recent events is sometimes known as 'recency'. Other problems include:

O appraising only the more obvious and describable elements of performance at the expense of the less easily definable but just as important ones;

O avoiding the high and low extremes on a rating scale and concentrating scores in the middle (central tendency);

O allowing past appraisals to influence the present appraisal;

O being over-influenced by easily observable events;

○ accepting other people's opinions about the individual too readily;

○ accepting without due consideration individuals at their own valuation.

This problem can be addressed by ensuring through training and guidance that appraisers base their judgements on observations or evidence about performance in relation to defined objectives and standards – the evidence preferably being derived by the use of valid performance measures. Competence frameworks or behaviourally anchored rating scales as described in Chapter 8 can provide reference points to assist in making more reliable and consistent judgements.

Interaction between the appraiser and the appraisee

Assessments are made on the basis both of observation during the course of normal day-to day work and the points emerging during the appraisal discussion. But their validity may be affected by the following problems:

○ *Poor perception* – not noticing things or events for what they are.

○ *Wishful thinking* – noticing only those things one wants to see.

○ *Poor interpretation* – putting one's own incorrect interpretation on information.

○ *projection* – seeing one's own faults in other people.

These problems can be overcome by adopting an analytical approach which dispassionately sifts all the evidence and comes to a rational conclusion on what it means. Empathy – the ability to match emotional responses and thus understand other people's behaviour or attitudes from their point of view – is required to obtain an accurate interpretation of why they are acting or reacting in a certain way. Some people are better than others in being analytical and in using empathy and that is why they are better and more reliable judges. But it is possible to develop these skills through training and this should always be part of the programmes for introducing performance appraisal and ensuring that it continues to operate effectively.

Stereotyping

Judgements are affected by the universal tendency to stereotype. We all tend to carry around with us a collection of mental pictures of what we imagine certain people to be like. Familiar stereotypes include curates, market traders and students. It is difficult to avoid stereotyping people as typical accountants, sales representatives or personnel managers, but appraisers should be encouraged as part of their training to control the tendency to stereotype because it is only when they can learn to see people as individuals that they are able to make an objective assessment of performance.

LACK OF SKILL IN CONDUCTING APPRAISAL DISCUSSIONS

Conducting performance appraisal discussions and making judgements about performance require skill, but no more than any good manager can develop with a little help. Poor managers and those who have not received adequate training can easily make mistakes like these:

○ Antagonising appraisees from the start by making critical comments.

○ Allowing the meeting to drift in a formless way.

○ Rushing the meeting through, giving a clear impression that this is something that has to be got over quickly.

○ Concentrating on blaming people for mistakes rather than working towards a solution.

○ Talking too much.

○ Failing to recognise that appraisal is a two way process, not an inquisition or exposition conducted by the appraiser.

O Not listening attentively.

O Not probing sufficiently to get to the bottom of a problem.

O Spending too much time looking backwards rather than forwards.

O Allowing the appraisee to dominate the proceedings.

O Avoiding the issue of poor performance because of a wish to avoid unpleasantness, either during or after the meeting.

O Making accusations without backing them up with evidence.

O Springing criticism on the appraisee for a past failure which had not been mentioned at the time.

O Reacting over-defensively if the appraisee makes a critical comment about the appraiser.

O Asking leading or rhetorical questions.

O Failing to check the understanding of the appraisee about a point that has been made.

O Failing to recap the main points emerging from the discussion to check that the appraiser's impressions correspond with those of the appraisee.

O Imposing solutions on appraisees, ignoring the fact that they will probably have ideas of their own which should be listened to.

O Not concluding a clear agreement with the appraisee about the way forward.

There seem to be an awful lot of problems but there are none that cannot be overcome with a little care. This should be exercised on the basis of an understanding that these sort of mistakes are easily made and can seriously prejudice the success of the meeting, coupled with training on ways to avoid them.

Research conducted by the Huthwaite Research Group as quoted in *Strategies for Human Resource Management* (edited by Michael Armstrong, Kogan Page, 1992) has shown that some behaviours are more effective than others, as the analysis of the behaviour used by 'average' and 'expert' appraisers as shown in Table 11.1.

Behaviour category	Behaviour used by 'average' reviewers	Behaviour used by 'expert' reviewers
Proposing	16.2	8.1
Building	1.8	4.7
Supporting	8.3	11.7
Disagreeing	6.8	7.2
Defend/attack	1.2	0.2
Testing understanding	3.1	8.3
Summarising	2.3	6.4
Seeking information	12.7	15.1
Seeking proposals	2.0	6.4
Giving information	33.5	17.0
Disclosing	12.0	14.9
	100.0	100.0

Table 11.1 *Approaches of average and expert reviewers*

This data demonstrates a number of important differences between the behaviour of 'expert' and 'average' reviewers. For instance, the average appraiser spends twice as long as the expert *giving information*. Moreover, by adding *giving information* to *proposing*, it appears that 50 per cent of the average appraiser's behaviour consists of giving opinions and ideas to subordinates. This compares with 20 per cent for the expert. Experts ask more questions. There are three behaviours which involve asking questions: *testing understanding, seeking information* and *testing proposals*. Added together, the figures for the expert are much higher – 29.8 per cent, compared with 17.8 per cent for the average appraiser.

The balance of questions differs. Of the average reviewer's 17.8 per cent, the majority consist of *seeking information*, while experts have a much greater proportion of *testing understanding* and *seeking proposals*. This suggests that experts are interested in what the appraisee 'thinks' and that they want to check that they have understood what is being said. Average appraisers, in contrast, are more interested in questioning appraisees directly. Experts spend more time clarifying the content of the discussion and provide more encouragement. They *build* as well as *propose* and offer more *support*. The expert's figure for *disagreeing* is slightly higher, showing that experts are by no means 'soft touches' – when they disagree, they say so.

Problems in Agreeing Objectives

Defining and agreeing objectives which meet the 'SMART' criteria as defined on page 43 is not always as easy as it seems. It may be difficult to find quantifiable objectives which can be reviewed against reliable and readily available performance measures. Qualitative standards may be difficult to draw up and even when an attempt to do so has been made, the result can become so bland that it is meaningless as a basis for assessing performance (although the process of working through the standard can be enlightening in itself).

This is another aspect of performance appraisal where training to both parties is essential and follow-up actions are required to check on how the objective setting and review sessions have gone is equally valuable.

SUMMARY

To summarise, the key points to which attention should be given to overcome the sort of problems described in this chapter are set out in the following checklists.

Appraisal Discussion Checklist

1. Try to be relaxed and put the appraisee at ease.
2. Outline the objectives, agenda and time allowed for the discussion.

3. Use the structure of:
   — current performance;
   — future targets;
   — development opportunities;
   (but be flexible to the needs of the appraisee).
4. Invite the appraisee to give their views before you give yours.
5. Keep to the facts; do not let bias cloud your judgement.
6. Use your interpersonal skills:
   — listen more than you speak;
   — keep the discussion positive;
   — focus on problem solving rather than apportioning blame;
   — focus on behaviour rather than personality;
   — be assertive, not aggressive;
   — use open questions to encourage the flow of information and discussion;
   — use probing questions to investigate deeper issues ;
   — be open to criticism;
   — be sensitive to underlying issues and concerns;
   — summarise and agree understanding regularly.
7. Agree and set 'SMART' objectives.
8. Summarise action points and end on a positive note.
9. Agree and record the key points of the discussion.
10. Ensure that you complete the actions to which you have agreed.

Reviews checklist

1. Agree appropriate time-scales for reviews.
2. Monitor progress against objectives and be alert to any potential problems.
3. Help appraisees to find their own solutions to problems.
4. Keep the channels of communication open.
5. Be supportive and encouraging.
6. Recognise and reward achievements.

Part 4

ACTION THROUGHOUT THE YEAR

12

The Continuing Process of Appraisal

Perhaps one of the most important features of the best approaches to performance appraisal is that it is a continuous affair which reflects normal good management practices of setting direction, monitoring and measuring performance and taking action accordingly. Performance appraisal should not be imposed on managers as something 'special' they have to do. It should be treated as a natural process which all good managers carry out. The sequence of performance appraisal activities as described in this book does no more than provide a framework within which managers, individuals and teams work together in whatever ways best suit them to gain better understanding of what is to be done, how it is to be done and what has been achieved. This framework and the philosophy that supports it can form the basis for training newly appointed or would-be managers in this key area of their responsibilities. It can also help in improving the performance of managers who are not up to standard in this respect.

Old fashioned performance appraisal schemes were usually built around an annual event, the formal review, which tended to dwell on the past. This was carried out at the behest of the personnel department, often perfunctorily, and then forgotten. Managers proceeded to manage without any further reference to the outcome of the review and the appraisal form was buried in the personnel record system.

A formal, often annual discussion, is still an important part of a performance appraisal system but it is not the most important part. Equal, if not more, prominence should be given to the continuing process of performance appraisal.

MANAGING PERFORMANCE THROUGHOUT THE YEAR

Performance appraisal should be regarded as an integral part of the continuing process of performance management. This is based on a philosophy which emphasises:

O the achievement of sustained improvements in performance;

O continuous development of skills and overall competence;

O that the organisation is a 'learning organisation' as described later in this chapter.

Managers and individuals should therefore be ready, willing and able to define and meet development and improvement needs as they arise. As far as practicable, learning and work should be integrated. This means that encouragement should be given to all managers and members of staff to learn from the successes, challenges and problems inherent in their day-to-day work.

The process of continuing assessment should be carried out by reference to agreed objectives and to work, development and improvement plans. Progress reviews can take place informally or through an existing system of team meetings. But there should be more formal interim reviews at predetermined points in the year, eg quarterly. For some teams or individual jobs these points could be related to 'milestones' contained in project and work plans. Deciding when such meetings should take place would be up to individual managers in consultation with their staff and would not be a laid-down part of a 'system'.

Managers would be encouraged to consider how to accommodate the need for regular dialogue within the established pattern of briefings, team or group meetings or project review meetings.

In addition to the collective meetings, managers may have regular one-to-one meetings with their staff. If performance appraisal is to be effective, there needs to be a continuing agenda through these regular meetings to ensure that good progress is being made towards achieving the objectives agreed for each key result area.

During these interim meetings, progress in achieving agreed operational and personal objectives and associated work, development and improvement plans, can be reviewed. As necessary, objectives and plans are revised.

Interim appraisal discussions should be conducted along the lines of the main appraisal discussions as described in Part 3. Any specific outcomes of the meeting should be recorded as amendments to the original agreement and objectives and plans.

The issues which may arise in the course of managing performance throughout the year are:

○ updating objectives;
○ continuous learning;
○ creating a learning organisation;
○ managing under-performers;
○ taking disciplinary action.

UPRATING OBJECTIVES AND WORK PLANS

The agreements about objectives and improvement plans made at a formal appraisal discussion are working documents. New demands, new situations arise, and provision therefore needs to be made for updating or amending objectives and work plans. This means:

○ discussing what the job holder has done and achieved;
○ identifying any shortfalls in achieving objectives or meeting standards;
○ establishing the reasons for any shortfalls, in particular examining changes in the circumstances in which the job is carried out, identifying new demands and pressures and considering aspects of the behaviour of the individual or the manager which have contributed to the problem;

○ agreeing any changes required to objectives and work plans in response to changed circumstances;

○ agreeing any actions required by the individual or the manager to improve performance.

MANAGING CONTINUOUS LEARNING

Performance appraisal aims to enhance what Alan Mumford (*Management Development; Strategies for Action*, IPM, 1989) calls deliberate learning from experience. This means learning from the problems, challenges and successes inherent in people's day-to-day activities.

The premiss is that every task individuals undertake presents them with a learning opportunity, as long as they reflect on what they have done and how they have done it and draw conclusions as to their future behaviour if they have to carry out a similar task. This principle can be extended to any situation when managers instruct subordinates or agree with them what needs to be achieved, followed by a review, which may be quite informal, of how well the task was accomplished. Such day-to-day contacts provide training as well as learning opportunities, and performance appraisal schemes emphasise that these should be deliberate acts. In other words, that managers, with their teams and the individual members of their team, should consciously agree on the lessons learned from experience and how this experience could be put to good use in the future.

For example, a team with the manager as project leader has the task of developing and implementing a new computerised system for responding to customer account queries. The team would start by jointly assessing with their leader their terms of reference, the project schedule, the budget and the results they are expected to deliver. The team would then analyse progress and at periodical 'milestone' meetings would review what has or has not been achieved, agree the lessons learned and decide on any actions to be taken in the shape of modifications to the way in which they conduct the project for the future. Learning is an implicit part of these reviews because the team will be deciding on any changes it should make to its method of operation – learning can be defined as the modification of behaviour through experience. The team would continue to adapt their behaviour as required and at the end of the project the team members would agree, with their leader, what lessons have been learned and affirm how they need to behave in the future on the basis of this review.

The same approach would apply to individuals. For example, the regional director of a large charity holds a monthly meeting with each of her field officers. At the meeting progress is reviewed and problems discussed. Successes would be analysed to increase the field officer's understanding of what needs to be done to repeat the successful performance in the future. If something has gone wrong the field officer could be asked to assess why that had happened and what needs to be done to avoid a re-occurrence of the problem.

There are examples of project or periodical work reviews. But continuous learning can take place even less formally, as when a team leader in an accounts department instructs an accounts assistant on his or her role in analysing management information from the final assembly department as part of a newly introduced activity based costing system. The instructions will cover what has to be done and how, and the team leader will later check that things are going according to plan. This will provide an opportunity for further learning on the part of the accounts assistant, prompted by the team leader, in any aspect of the task where problems have occurred in getting it done properly.

CREATING A LEARNING ORGANISATION

A learning organisation can be defined by as one which facilitates the learning of all its members and continually transforms itself. In *The Age of Unreason* (Business Books, 1989) Charles Handy describes a learning organisation as one that both learns and encourages learning in people. It creates space for people to question, think and learn, and constantly reframes the world and their part in it. The learning organisation, according to Handy, needs to have a formal way of asking questions, seeking out theories and reflecting on them. Members of the organisation must be encouraged to challenge traditional ways of doing things and suggest improvements.

All successful companies are good at doing certain things. This is their knowledge and skills base. This base must be developed to match changing conditions. Learning is not just the acquisition of new knowledge; it is rather a collective process of observation, experimentation and experience which can be mobilised to deal with new opportunities or threats.

It is necessary for companies to 'make space' in meetings, workshops and conferences so that people can reflect on what they have learned and need to learn. But what needs to be learned cannot always be taught. Performance appraisal therefore, must, help people to learn from their experience. Learning cannot be left to chance.

The characteristics of a learning organisation are that it:

O encourages people to identify and satisfy their own learning needs;

O provides individuals with regular reviews of performance and learning needs;

O provides feedback on performance and achieved learning;

O provides new experiences from which people can learn;

O facilitates the use of training on the job.

IMPROVING PERFORMANCE

It has been estimated by Philip Atkinson ('Managing Performance', *Managing Service Quality*, March, 1992) that on average, 10 to 25 per cent of all employees are under-performing. So what needs to be done?

The approach to managing under-performers should be based on reinforcement theory. As Charles Handy (ibid) has put it, this is about 'applauding success and forgiving failure'. He suggests that mistakes should be used as an opportunity for learning – 'something only possible if the mistake is *truly* forgiven because otherwise the lesson is heard as a reprimand and not as an offer of help'.

Managing under-performers is therefore a positive process which is based on feedback throughout the year and looks forward to what can be done by individuals to overcome performance problems and, importantly, how managers can help.

The five basic steps required to manage under-performers are:

1. **Identify and agree the problem.** Analyse the feedback and, as far as possible, obtain agreement from the individual on what the shortfall has been. Feedback may be provided by managers but it should be built into the job. This takes place when individuals are aware of their targets and standards, know what performance measures will be used and either receive feedback/control information automatically or have easy access to it. They will then be in a position to measure and assess their own performance and, if they are well-motivated and well-trained, take their own corrective actions. In other words, a self-regulating feedback mechanism exists. This is a situation which managers should endeavour to create on the grounds that prevention is better than cure.

2. **Establish the reason(s) for the shortfall.** When seeking the reasons for any shortfalls the manager should not crudely be trying to attach blame. The aim should be for the manager and the individual jointly to identify the facts that have contributed to the problem. It is on the basis of this factual analysis that decisions can be made on what to do about it by the individual, the manager or the two of them working together.

   It is necessary first to identify any causes which are external to the job and outside the control of either the manager or the individual. Any factors which are within the control of the individual and/or the manager can then be considered.

An example of a checklist used by an organisation to analyse factors affecting managerial performance is given in Appendix C and a checklist for analysing performance problems is given in Appendix D.

3. **Decide and agree on the action required.** Action may be taken by the individual, the manager or both parties. This could include:

— taking steps to improve skills or change behaviour – the individual;

— changing attitudes – this is up to individuals as long as they accept that their attitudes need to be changed;

— providing more support or guidance – the manager;

— clarifying expectations – joint;

— developing abilities and skills – joint, in the sense that individuals may be expected to take steps to develop themselves but managers may provide help in the form of coaching, additional experience or training.

Whatever action is agreed both parties must understand how they will know that it has succeeded. Feedback arrangements can be made but individuals should be encouraged to monitor their own performance and take further action as required.

4. **Resource the action.** Provide the coaching, training, guidance, experience or facilities required to enable agreed actions to happen.

5. **Monitor and provide feedback** Both managers and individuals monitor performance, ensure that feedback is provided or obtained and analysed, and agree on any further actions that may be necessary.

Checklists for Managing Under-Performers

The following checklists set out the questions which can usefully be answered when dealing with different aspects of substandard performance.

Failure to Achieve Objectives or Standards

○ To what extent have objectives not been achieved?

○ What specific instances have there been of substandard performance?

○ Did the individual fully understand what he/she was expected to achieve?

○ Were these expectations reasonable in the light of the individual's experience and qualifications to do the job?

○ Did the way in which the job was structured contribute to the failure?

○ Did the individual get sufficient support from his/her manager or team leader and the other members of the team?

○ Was the individual aware that his/her work was not up to standard and what, if anything, was he/she doing about it?

○ Was the problem caused by inadequate knowledge or lack of skill in any respect?

○ To what extent, if any, was the failure to achieve targets or meet performance standards simply because of a lack of effort or interest on the part of the individual?

The answers to these questions should provide some indication of the action that could be taken, for example:

○ clarifying objectives and standards;

○ reformulating objectives to make them attainable (but not too easily);

○ redesigning the job (adjusting tasks and responsibilities) to provide a sounder basis for obtaining better results;

○ re-examining the composition of the team and its methods of working followed, if necessary, by a team-building programme;

○ improving the feedback on results to the individual, and monitoring performance following the feedback to ensure that corrective action is taken as necessary;

O encouraging the individuals to develop the additional knowledge or skills themselves while providing guidance and coaching as required;

O if a self-development approach is inappropriate or insufficient, arranging for specific training or coaching in areas where deficiencies in knowledge or skill have been identified;

O helping individuals to learn from their mistakes, thus knowing how to minimise the risk of repeating them;

O encouraging individuals to recognise that certain aspects of their behaviour have contributed to the substandard results and getting them to agree to the achievement of specified modifications in behaviour.

The last action is probably the most difficult one to carry out successfully.

A checklist for handling unacceptable attitudes and behaviour is set out below.

Handling Attitude and Behavioural Problems

O Why do you believe that there is a problem over the employee's attitudes or behaviour?

O What evidence do you have that the attitude/behaviour is creating a performance problem? (Quote actual examples).

O Have you discussed with the individual at the time any instance of poor performance which you believe could be attributed to negative attitudes or behaviour?

O How did the individual react when asked to comment on any such instances?

O What steps have you taken to enable the employee to recognise his/her own problem or situation and discuss it with you?

O Have you taken into account the fact that in general it is easier to change behaviour than deep-seated attitudes?

O Have you been successful in obtaining agreement on the cause of the problem and what should be done about it?

O If so, have you agreed how the problem should be managed by the individual with whatever help you and, possibly, other people could provide?

O If not, is this a problem which you would refer to another counselling source (eg a member of the human resource department) for resolution?

The approach described above requires the manager to act as a counsellor rather than as an authoritarian figure handing out threats or promises of reward. Counselling is a skilled process and managers need to be convinced of its value as a means of managing performance and trained in how to do it (Chapter 13 deals with counselling techniques in more detail).

There will, unfortunately, be situations when counselling does not work. The problem persists, the employee is incorrigible, and the disciplinary procedure has to be invoked, as discussed in the last section of this chapter.

Unwillingness to Accept Objectives or Standards

The 'management by contract' aspect of performance appraisal is basic to its philosophy, but what happens if someone does not agree to what the manager believes to be entirely fair although possibly stretching objectives or standards? The following questions need to be addressed by the manager in this situation:

O How certain am I that this is an attainable objective or standard?

O Have I any 'benchmarking' evidence that targets or standards of this nature have been achieved by other people in similar circumstances?

O Is it reasonable for me to ask this particular individual to achieve this objective or standard in the light of his/her experience or qualifications or the circumstances in which the job is carried out?

O Does the individual have any reasonable grounds for rejecting the objective or standard?

○ If not, why is he/she adopting this attitude?

○ Do I insist on this objective or standard in spite of the individual's objections?

○ If not, to what extent am I prepared to modify the objective?

In the last analysis, if you believe that an objective or standard is essential and attainable you have to insist on it. It may be one which has to be achieved if you are going to reach objectives or standards to which you have already agreed as being proper and reasonable. And if, for example, the business will not survive unless certain targets for earnings per share or return on capital employed are achieved, you cannot agree to an individual target which is not going to make an adequate contribution to the overall result required. There may be some discussion about how it is to be achieved but there can be no dispute over the fact that it must be achieved if at all possible.

The same principle applies to performance standards. If, for example, you know that you will lose valuable customers if you cannot guarantee a proper response to an enquiry within 24 hours and also know that the resources are available to achieve that standard, then it is entirely reasonable to insist on it, even though you may have to accept that it cannot be achieved overnight (but spell out when it has to be reached).

The aim is, of course, to avoid an impasse, and if you have difficulty in reaching agreement you have to do your best to persuade the individual that the target or standard is reasonable, promising any necessary help if that is appropriate.

If this does not work you may allow the employee to appeal to a higher authority (eg your boss). If such an appeal is not upheld you would have no alternative but to insist on the target or standard you require and you would have to inform the individual that you expect that every effort will be made to reach it. If subsequently, and without good reason, the individual fails to achieve the target or standard you would then have to consider taking one of the following actions: issuing an informal warning as the first stage in a disciplinary procedure, requesting that the individual is transferred to another job, or restructuring the present job to fit the individual's capabilities. The latter action could involve regrading and a reduction in pay and might therefore have to be carried out through the disciplinary procedure.

It is to be hoped that such situations will seldom, if ever, arise, but what you cannot afford to do is allow substandard performance to continue unchecked. Performance appraisal essentially involves management by agreement, but if that agreement is unreasonably withheld managers have to exert their authority in order to get the job done well.

PERFORMANCE APPRAISAL AND DISCIPLINE

Performance appraisal is a positive process and that is why a counselling approach is desirable when faced with substandard performance, although this should be adopted at the time the problem occurs rather than being saved up for a formal and intimidating meeting.

If counselling fails to improve the situation it may, unfortunately, be necessary to leave the performance appraisal process and enter the disciplinary procedure. This should start with an informal warning, followed by a formal written warning if the informal warning is not heeded and, as a last resort, dismissal or some other disciplinary action.

Warnings should always spell out the problem and indicate as specifically as possible what the employee has to do or how he/she is expected to behave to avoid the invocation of the next stage of the disciplinary procedure. The employee should be given every chance to respond to the warning and should be allowed to appeal against it if, in spite of his/her objections, the warning is confirmed. Help in the form of further counselling, coaching or training should be offered wherever possible – the aims are to ensure that the informal warning will overcome the problem and that no further disciplinary action has to be taken.

Although disciplinary action can be used as a means of overcoming performance problems it should be treated as a separate procedure which is not regarded as part of the normal processes of performance management. These processes may help to identify performance problems which they will deal with on the spot, if at all possible. Only if this fails are these problems transferred to the disciplinary system for resolution.

This separation of performance appraisal processes and disciplinary procedures is important because of the serious harm that would be done to the positive performance improvement and developmental aspects of performance appraisal if employees felt that the process was simply being used to collect evidence for use in taking disciplinary action. Performance discussions can become threatening affairs if they are perceived simply as opportunities for managers to obtain evidence which can be used against their staff.

If the problem has to be transferred to the disciplinary procedure for resolution it is highly desirable to state what it is in full, with any supporting evidence which is available. Reference can be made to the fact that the problem was identified earlier as part of the continuing process of performance appraisal but the content of any record of a performance appraisal discussion should not be used as evidence. The disciplinary warning must be complete in itself.

In practice this may not cause much difficulty as long as the manager follows the guidelines for managing performance throughout the year as described above. These suggest that immediate action is taken to deal with performance problems – they should not be saved up to be discussed at a formal appraisal meeting some time after the event. Raising problems immediately means that they are dealt with as a normal management process, and the disciplinary procedure should only be resorted to when this process fails, in spite of every effort to make it succeed.

13

Coaching and Counselling

One of the principal aims of performance appraisal, if not the principal aim, is to help people to help themselves. This is best done through coaching and counselling. In many ways appraisers primarily act as coaches and counsellors, helpers, not judges.

COACHING

Coaching is a personal (usually one-to-one), on-the-job approach used by managers and trainers to help people develop their skills and levels of competence. As a manager, you are there to get results through people and this means that you have a personal responsibility for ensuring they acquire and develop the skills they need. Other people in the shape of training and management development specialists may help but because by far the best way of learning is on the job, the onus is mainly on you.

The need for coaching may arise from formal or informal performance appraisal discussions but opportunities for coaching will emerge during normal day-to-day activities. Every time you delegate a new task to someone a coaching opportunity is created to help the individual learn any new skills or techniques which are needed to get the job done. Every time you provide feedback to an individual after a task has been completed there is an opportunity to help that individual do better next time. Methods of giving feedback were described in Chapter 9.

The Coaching Process

Coaching consists of:

○ Making people aware of how well they are performing by, for example, asking them questions to establish the extent to which they have thought through what they are doing.

○ Controlled delegation – ensuring that individuals not only know what is expected of them but also understand what they need to know and be able to do to complete the task satisfactorily. This gives you an opportunity to provide guidance at the outset – guidance at a later stage may be seen as interference.

○ Using whatever situations which may arise as opportunities to promote learning.

○ Encouraging people to look at higher-level problems and how they would tackle them.

Coaching Skills

Coaching will be most effective when:

○ the coach understands that his or her role is to help people to learn;

○ individuals are motivated to learn – they should be aware that their present level of knowledge or skill or their behaviour needs to be improved if they are going to perform their work to their own and to others' satisfaction;

○ individuals are given guidance on what they should be learning and feedback on how they are doing;

○ learning is an active, not a passive process – individuals need to be actively involved with their coach;

○ the coach listens to individuals to understand what they want and need;

○ the coach adopts a constructive approach, building on strengths and experience.

Planned Coaching

Coaching may be informal but it has to be planned. It is not simply checking from time to time on what people are doing and then advising them on how to do it better. Nor is it occasionally telling people where they have gone wrong and throwing in a lecture for good measure. As far as possible, coaching should take place within the framework of a general plan of the areas and direction in which individuals will benefit from further development. Coaching plans can and should be incorporated into the general development plans set out at the end of an appraisal discussion, as described in Chapter 10.

The Manager as Coach

Coaching enables you to provide motivation, structure and effective feedback as long as you have the required skills and commitment. As coaches, good managers believe that people can succeed and that they can contribute to their success. They can identify what people need to be able to do to improve their performance. They have to see this as an important part of the role – an enabling, empowering process which focuses on learning requirements.

COUNSELLING

Counselling has been described by the Institute of Personnel and Development (IPD) (*Statement on Counselling in the Workplace*, 1992) as: 'Any activity in the workplace where one individual uses a set of skills and techniques to help another individual to take responsibility for and to manage their own decision-making whether it is work related or personal'.

Counselling is central to the management and development of people. All managers engage in some activity which could be termed as counselling as part of their normal working life. It is therefore a natural component of management – an everyday activity which can arise from immediate feedback.

One of your important aims as a manager is to get individuals to accept much of the responsibility for their own self-development. What people seek out for themselves, with some guidance as necessary, is likely to make a greater impact than anything handed out to them by their managers or by a trainer. Of course, you still have to make clear your expectations of what individuals have to achieve. And it is also necessary to ensure that they have the necessary training and guidance to enable them to meet your expectations. There will also be occasions when you have to spell out how you expect the job or task to be done. But you will make no progress in developing the skills and abilities of your staff if you only tell them how to do things or how they should solve their work problems. Your job is to do as much as you can to help them to help themselves, because that is the best way for them to learn.

The Counselling Process

The counselling process as described by the IPD consists of three stages:

O **Recognition and understanding** – recognising the indicators of problems and issues.

O **Empowering** – enabling the employee to recognise his or her own problem or situation and encouraging them to express it.

O **Resourcing** – managing the problem, which will include the decision on who is best able to act as counsellor – the manager, the specialist or an outside resource.

Approaches to Counselling

One of the best known methods of counselling was described by Norman Maier some time ago (*The Appraisal Interview*, Wiley, 1958). He suggested that there were three approaches available in a performance appraisal meeting:

1. *The tell and sell approach* in which appraisers seek first to let appraisees know how they are doing, then gain their acceptance of the evaluation and, finally, get them to follow a plan outlined for their improvement. The problem with this method is that considerable skill is required to get people to accept criticisms delivered in this way and to change in the

required manner. There are occasions when people have to be told what to do, but it may not always be possible to provide the motivation for change, unless resort is made to crude inducements or threats.

2. *The tell and listen approach* in which the evaluation is communicated to appraisees who are then allowed to respond to it. Instead of appraisers dominating the discussion they sit back and become non-directive counsellors during the second part of the meeting. Appraisees are encouraged to think things out for themselves and to decide on what needs to be done. The assumption is made that they are more likely to change in these circumstances than if they had been told what to do. An advantage of this approach is that appraisers can profit more from the discussion by receiving feedback from appraisees on how improvements can be achieved with regard to management, work methods, the provision of resources, dealing with problems outside the control of appraisees and job assignments. However, this method also requires skill on the part of appraisers in listening, reflecting feelings and summarising opinions.

3. *The problem-solving approach* – this requires appraisers to start by encouraging appraisees to identify problem areas and then exchange ideas about solutions. Appraisees therefore play an active part in reviewing problem areas and in deciding what should be done about them. The evaluation of performance emerges from this discussion rather than being imposed on appraisees. In this approach the emphasis is less on what went right or wrong with performance in the past and more on ensuring that steps are taken to improve performance in the future. According to Maier, this method motivates original thinking and provides the intrinsic motivation that can be derived from the work itself and the process of overcoming work problems. Job satisfaction can be improved by reorganising or enriching the job, by changing the appraisees' perception of their role and by increasing the appraisers' ability to provide guidance and help in the form it is needed.

Again this approach needs skill but it is the most fruitful method and Maier recommends that appraisers should adopt it and abandon the 'tell and sell' and 'tell and listen' methods.

Counselling Stages

In *The Skilled Helper: A Systematic Guide to Effective Helping* (Brooks Cole, 1990) G. Egan has suggested that the stages to be followed in counselling are:

1. *Listening, understanding and communicating*. This focuses on understanding the perspective of the other person and communicating that understanding. It is non-judgemental and concentrates on ensuring that both parties have the same understanding of the situation.

2. *Changing the picture*. Talking through an issue can help to change appraisees' perspectives and indicate a solution to the problem. But this does not always happen and as a counsellor, you may have to use the 'tougher' skills of challenging and confronting, sharing with appraisees their different perceptions and providing a different framework. The initial listening phase should have established an atmosphere of acceptance and openness which enables this tougher stage to take the process forward into action.

3. *Implementing action*. In this stage you resource the individual to take action. You become a facilitator, helping the individual to formulate action plans and providing expertise and guidance as necessary. However, it is not your role as a counsellor to tell the individual what action to take. The individual must be helped to work out for himself or herself what needs to be done and how it should be done, although you should provide the resources required in the shape of coaching, training or the provision of better working facilities or systems. You can also be available to provide any additional guidance or help the individual requires.

Counselling Skills

The counselling skills you need to develop are:

○ **Problem identification** – recognising that the problem exists.

○ **Open questioning** – probing by open-ended, non-directive questions to identify the real focus of the problem rather than concentrating on its symptoms.

○ **Listening** – the ability to listen actively to obtain the full story by probing, evaluating, interpreting and supporting.

○ **Sensitivity** – to individual beliefs and values, some of which may be based on culture or religion.

○ **Reflecting** – being able to restate the problem from the individual's point of view.

○ **Empathy** – having regard for the feelings and anxieties of the individual.

○ **Impartiality** – the ability to remain non-judgemental and to refrain from prescribing solutions.

○ **Sincerity** – having a genuine attitude of interest and openness to the individual's problems.

○ **Belief** – having the belief that individuals have the resources to solve their own problems, albeit with passive or active help.

Effective counselling requires the use of skills which few managers are likely to acquire in the normal course of their work. It is essential, therefore, that training should be given to appraisers on how to counsel during formal and informal discussions. Counselling skills are best developed by practice under guidance and such guidance is a requisite part of any good performance appraisal scheme.

Part 5

DEVELOPING, INTRODUCING AND OPERATING PERFORMANCE APPRAISAL

14

Developing Performance Appraisal

Although the emphasis throughout this book has been on performance appraisal as a natural process of management rather than a 'system' it is still necessary to define the processes involved. This provides a framework within which appraisers and appraisees can operate and a basis for defining the approaches they should use and the skills training they require to obtain the maximum benefit from appraisal.

A development programme for performance appraisal can be carried out in the following stages:

1. Determine overall approach to performance appraisal.
2. Decide how and where to introduce performance appraisal.
3. Decide who is to be covered.
4. Decide on whether or not the same approach should be adopted at each level.
5. Set up project team.
6. Define role of human resources department.
7. Decide on whether or not to use outside consultants.
8. Define performance management processes and documentation including rating systems.
9. Pilot test and make amendments as necessary.
10. Plan implementation programme.

OVERALL APPROACH

The decisions on the overall approach to introducing performance appraisal should cover the points listed below. These points also could apply when it is proposed radically to change an existing method of performance appraisal.

1. What are our objectives in introducing performance appraisal?
2. What are the benefits anticipated from introducing performance appraisal?
3. What are the main features of the approach to performance appraisal which should be developed covering:
    — roles of appraisers and appraisees;
    — use of objectives and competences as the basis for appraisal;
    — types of performance agreements and development plans to be used;
    — methods of conducting appraisal discussions;
    — how often appraisal discussions should be held – many organisations carry these out annually but others arrange for half-yearly or even quarterly discussions;
    — rating systems;
    — documentation;
    — links, if any, to performance-related pay;
    — ensuring that performance appraisal is a continuous process;
    — training in appraisal skills;
    — monitoring application of appraisal?

WHERE AND HOW SHOULD PERFORMANCE APPRAISAL BE INTRODUCED?

Performance appraisal is best introduced on an organisation-wide basis, starting at the top. In most cases the philosophy, principles and key procedures and processes are developed centrally.

In a highly decentralised organisation, separate business units may be allowed to decide for themselves whether or not they want performance appraisal and if they do, develop it on their own.

An intermediate approach adopted by some decentralised organisations is for the centre (top management) to require all divisions and business units to introduce performance appraisal in accordance with certain general principles which the centre lays down. The business units proceed to develop their own processes, but the centre provides help as required and may monitor the introduction of performance appraisal in each division to ensure that it is happening according to plan and in line with corporate principles and values.

The most common and best method of introduction is to set up a project team or working group for this purpose with management and staff representatives. This provides for different opinions and experiences to be considered, serves as a base for wider consultation and communications to take place and generally helps to achieve ownership. The operation of project teams is discussed in the next section of this chapter.

There may be a central project team to draw up the basic principles of performance appraisal but some organisations have also provided for the full involvement of line management and employees by introducing it progressively in each major division or function. The management team of the department acts as its own working group and decides in full consultation with members of the department how it will operate. A series of workshops may be held within the division or department to brief and train managers and staff. Assistance will be given to this development programme by members of the central project team or the human resources department and/or an external consultant. This approach is also designed to enhance ownership – the aim is to get each division or department to believe that this is their scheme which fits into their normal pattern of working (objective setting, planning and reviewing).

HOW OFTEN SHOULD PERFORMANCE APPRAISAL TAKE PLACE?

The most typical arrangement is for there to be one formal appraisal discussion a year. Some schemes require formal discussions to take place twice or even four times a year. The fact that there is only an annual appraisal does not mean that interim 'milestone' meetings might be held and these are, in fact, highly desirable, especially when the objectives include the introduction of major projects.

Most organisations lay down that there should be an annual or half-yearly review but encourage their managers to have further reviews as they feel fit.

WHO SHOULD BE COVERED?

Another important decision to be made at the outset is who should be covered by performance appraisal. At one time most schemes were restricted to managers but performance appraisal is now more generally being extended to all professional, administrative, technical and support staff. Some organisations also include shopfloor workers, especially high tech firms, those that rely on production by high performance work teams, companies with integrated pay structures and terms and conditions of employment (often high tech and/or international firms) and companies with performance-related pay for manual workers.

DIFFERENT APPROACHES ACCORDING TO LEVEL?

If performance appraisal does cover managers and professional/ technical staff, administrative, clerical and support staff and, possibly manual workers, a decision has to be made on whether or not the same approach should be used for everybody.

Many organisations believe that it would be invidious to distinguish between levels so far as the essence of the approach is concerned, although they might accept that different performance measures may be used. For example, at the highest level performance would be assessed almost entirely in relation to quantified targets. At other levels and in jobs where quantified targets are difficult to fix, there may be an increasing emphasis on assessment in relation to qualitative performance standards and competences.

Some organisations do distinguish between roles where quantified and regularly updated short-term objectives will be set and those where continuing performance standards are more usual. In the former case they may refer to the key result areas of the job as 'principal accountabilities'; in the latter they may use terms such as 'main tasks' or 'key activities'.

It may also be recognised that the objective setting and appraisal process in more routine jobs may not need to be as exhaustive as for those in managerial or professional roles.

PROJECT TEAMS

As mentioned above, project teams consisting of managers and other employees and facilitated by a member of the human resources department and/or outside consultant are a valuable means of getting involvement and ownership. The individual members of the team can be responsible not only for taking part in the development of performance appraisal but also for helping to introduce it in their own departments and for consulting with and communicating to their colleagues.

Project teams are likely to be advisory bodies in that they will present their recommendation to the board or a steering committee where the final decision will be made. But if the project team does its work well and ensures that the board or steering committee is given progress reports and the opportunity to comment as the project proceeds, it should not normally have any serious difficulty in getting its views accepted.

The project may be led by a senior member of the human resources department (often the human resources director) or a senior line manager. That person will not only have the responsibility for leading the team but also for communicating with the board and other senior colleagues to ensure that they are convinced that the project is proceeding in the right direction.

The project team should be briefed on why the organisation wants to introduce performance appraisal and the objectives they have set for it. They may be told that they are an advisory body, but the importance of their contribution to developing the scheme and helping to gain its acceptance should be emphasised.

The team should be given deadlines for each main stage of its work, eg:

1. Agree basic features of performance appraisal.
2. Develop details of processes and procedures and produce a description of the approach they recommend.
3. Pilot test.
4. Brief employees.
5. Develop and coordinate training.
6. Implement.
7. Evaluate.

An indication should also be made of when the team is expected to provide progress reports to management and to managers and employees generally and in what form such reports should be presented. It might be appropriate to require reports and review meetings after each of the main stages of the project.

If there are to be internal or external facilitators their role should be defined in advance. Basically, this could be to present ideas for the team to discuss, to bring to the attention of the team relevant information and lessons from experiences in other organisations, to record and present the outcome of the team's discussions in the form of draft descriptions of the process, and to draft documentation, briefing notes and training specification. The facilitator could also be involved in planning and conducting pilot schemes, training, monitoring implementation and evaluation.

ROLE OF THE HUMAN RESOURCES FUNCTION

The role of the human resources function in developing and implementing performance appraisal is initially to convince top management that its introduction will make a significant impact on the organisation's performance. It must then show the way to top management, line managers and employees generally. But it is not the role of the human resources function to bulldoze the organisation into introducing performance appraisal. As a human resources manager said to one of the IPD researchers on performance management (IPD 1992) 'our role has been to act as a searchlight, not a World War I tank'.

Members of the human resources function can play an important part in leading and facilitating project teams, in planning and implementing briefing and training programmes and in providing individual guidance, counselling and coaching to line managers. In effect, they can operate as internal consultants.

In one sense, the human resources function is the custodian of performance appraisal on behalf of top management. It has to ensure that it is operating effectively and it should exercise some form of quality control for that purpose. However, this role should be carried out with discretion. The function should not set out to exercise rigid, bureaucratic control, members of the function are there to facilitate appraisal not to police it. Follow-up and evaluation studies, including attitude surveys, may be the responsibility of the human resources function although it could work with a standing performance appraisal project team. There is much to be said for extending the development role of the team into one of monitoring performance appraisal in action.

It may or may not be thought desirable for the human resources function to be assisted by external consultants.

USE OF EXTERNAL CONSULTANTS

External consultants can be used to advise on and facilitate the introduction of performance appraisal, to run training programmes and to carry out evaluation studies, including the conduct of attitude surveys.

The advantage of using external consultants is that they can bring experience, expertise, independence and a useful 'extra pair of hands' to the project. They should be used to working with project teams and understand how best to facilitate their processes.

But they can be costly and care must be taken in selecting consultants who have the required level of experience and expertise and who, as far as can be judged, will 'fit' the culture of the organisation. It is also necessary to ensure that they are properly briefed and that firm programmes, timetables and cost budgets are agreed in advance and adhered to.

DEFINING PERFORMANCE APPRAISAL PROCESSES AND PROCEDURES

The answers to the questions listed above and the contents of previous chapters of this book will provide a sound basis for developing performance. The project team appraisal processes and procedures will need to pay attention to each point against a background of an understanding of the objectives to be attained and the culture and structure of the organisation. Particular attention will need to be given to the development of rating plans and document design.

Rating Plans

If it is decided that rating is necessary, and not all organisations believe that this is the case, decisions on the following factors will have to be made:

O negative as well as positive definitions;
O the number of levels in the scale.

Positive–Negative Definitions Traditionally, definitions have regressed downwards from a highly positive, eg 'exceptional' description to a negative, eg 'unsatisfactory' definition as in the following typical example:

A Outstanding performance in all respects.
B Superior performance, significantly above normal job requirements.

C Good all round performance which meets the normal requirements of the job.
D Performance not fully up to requirements. Clear weaknesses
   requiring improvement have been identified.
E Unacceptable; constant guidance is required and performance of
   many aspects of the job is well below a reasonable standard.

An alternative and increasingly popular approach is to have a
rating scale which provides positive reinforcement at every level.
This is in line with a culture of continuous improvement. The
example given below emphasises the positive and improvable
nature of individual performance.

Very effective	Meets all the objectives of the job. Exceeds required standards and consistently performs in a thoroughly proficient manner beyond normal expectations.
Effective	Achieves required objectives and standards of performance and meets the normal expectations of the job.
Developing	A contribution which is stronger in some aspects of the job than others, where most objectives are met but where performance improvements should still take place.
Basic	A contribution which on the whole meets the basic standards required although a number of objectives are not met and there is clearly room for improvement in several definable areas.

Positive definitions aim to avoid the use of terminology for
middle-ranking but entirely acceptable performers such as 'satisfactory' or 'competent' which seem to be damning people with
faint praise.

Some organisations use the term 'improvable' for the 'basic'
category on this list. Others have included 'learner/achiever' or
'unproven/too soon to tell' categories for new entrants to a grade
for whom it is too early to give a realistic assessment.

This scale deliberately avoids including an 'unacceptable' rating
or its equivalent on the grounds that if someone's performance is
totally unacceptable and not improvable, this should have been
identified during the continuous process of performance management and corrective action initiated at the time. This is not an

action that can be delayed for several months until the next review when a negative formal rating is given which may be too demotivating or too late. If such action fails to remedy the problem the employee may be dealt with under the disciplinary procedure and the normal performance review suspended unless and until the problem is overcome. However, the disciplinary procedure should still provide for performance reviews to assess the extent to which the requirements set out in the informal or formal warnings have been met.

Note also that in order to dispel any unfortunate associations with other systems such as school reports, this 'positive' scale does not include alphabetic or numerical ratings.

Number of Rating Levels   There has been much debate on what constitutes the 'best' number of rating levels. The normal practice is to have either four or five levels.

Four-level scales are frequently used, often with positive definitions as in the example given on page 181 although five-level scales are probably the most typical arrangement. They usually provide for two superior performance levels, a fully satisfactory level and two shades of less than competent performance. The definition of the lower two levels might be expressed more positively.

The rationale for five grades is that raters prefer this degree of fineness in performance definition and can easily recognise the middle grade and distinguish those who fall into higher or lower categories. However, when confronted with a five-level scale raters can be tempted to over-concentrate on the middle rating and avoid discriminating sufficiently between superior and inferior performers. Alternatively, five level scales can lead to 'rating drift' – a tendency to push ratings into higher categories. This can only be avoided by carefully wording the level descriptions to ensure that the middle category is used appropriately and by training managers in rating methodology.

The format to use is a matter of choice and judgement. No single approach is clearly much superior to another. It does, however, seem to be preferable for level definitions to be positive rather than negative and for them to provide a degree of reliable guidance on the choice of ratings. It is even more important to ensure that level definitions are compatible with the culture of the organisation and that close attention is given to ensuring that managers use them as consistently as possible.

Form Design

When designing performance appraisal forms the aim should be to keep them as simple and brief as possible while allowing ample 'white space' for comments. Like all good forms, they should be self-explanatory but they may be supplemented by notes for guidance.

Although documentation should be kept to a minimum such documents as are used should be well designed and presented. A typical set of forms which include an overall performance rating section is illustrated in Appendix B.

PILOT TESTS

There is much to be said for pilot testing at least some aspects of performance appraisal – bearing in mind that the usual cycle lasts 12 months and it may therefore be difficult to pilot test the whole process.

Examples of aspects of performance appraisal which can be tested are drawing up performance agreements, objective setting and document completion.

PREPARE BRIEFING PAPERS

It is desirable to issue an overall description of performance management to all employees which sets out its objectives and method of operation and the benefits it is expected to provide for the organisation and its managers and employees. Some organisations have prepared elaborate and lengthy briefing documents but fairly succinct documents often suffice as long as they are written in simple language and are well produced.

It is desirable to supplement written with oral briefings through a briefing group system, if there is one, or a special briefing programme. In a large or dispersed organisation this briefing will have to be carried out by line managers and they should be issued with special briefing packs and, possibly, a list of typical questions and their answers.

PLAN IMPLEMENTATION PROGRAMME

The implementation programme should cover the:

O date of introducing performance appraisal in the whole or different parts of the organisation (phased as necessary);

O briefing plan;

O training programme;

O procedure for evaluating the process.

15

Introducing and Operating Performance Appraisal

The introduction of performance appraisal should have been planned in the development stage. The main steps to take are to brief everyone as suggested in the last chapter and then implement a training programme. Once in operation it is essential to monitor and evaluate how performance appraisal is working out in practice.

TRAINING

The importance of thorough training for both appraisers and appraisees in the skills required to carry out performance appraisal effectively cannot be overemphasised. Many, if not most, of those involved will not consciously have practised the skills of objective setting, providing feedback, coaching and counselling. Both parties in the performance appraisal process also will need guidance and training in the use of competences, the preparation of performance agreements and plans, the preparation for and conduct of performance reviews, ratings and the completion of review forms. There is also, importantly, the need to develop the skills required to conduct appraisal discussions, including interpersonal skills. Again, it should be emphasised that, if at all possible, training should be extended to appraisees as well as appraisers.

Although some of these skills and procedures, such as providing feedback, coaching, counselling and rating will be practised mainly by managers, appraisees also need to know the part they have to play on the basis of an appreciation of what their managers are doing and why they are doing it.

Performance appraisal is concerned with content, ie the procedures for completing performance agreements and review forms, but more importantly it will be about process, setting objectives, using competence guidelines, defining attribute and competence levels, selecting and using performance measures and indicators and, of course, providing feedback, counselling and coaching.

Methods of Providing Training

Training can be provided by formal courses (as long as they are highly participative) or workshops. The objectives of the training could be set out as follows:

On completing the training those who participate should understand:

1. The aims and principles of performance appraisal.
2. The sequence of activities that will take place.
3. How to carry out or participate in the following processes:
— agreeing key tasks;
— setting objectives;
— agreeing skill, knowledge and competence requirements;
— appraisal discussions;
— reviewing performance on a continuing basis;
— providing feedback;
— counselling and coaching;
— preparing work and development plans.

Training Programmes

It is probably best to develop a series of training modules – it might be difficult to get people to go through all the training required at one time which in any case they would be unable to absorb. The modules could consist of:

1. Introduction to performance appraisal.
2. Defining key tasks and objective setting.

3. Working with attributes and competences – analysis and measurement.

4. Preparing work and development plans.

5. Conducting appraisal discussions.

6. Rating.

7. Providing feedback.

8. Coaching and counselling.

These modules could be combined in two programmes, each lasting at least a whole working day (if more time could be spared for practice and consolidation, so much the better).

The first programme could be designed to launch the scheme and would include modules one to four, ie a description of the process, defining key tasks, setting objectives and understanding competences and preparing work and development plans to produce a performance agreement.

The second programme could be run before formal discussions take place and would include modules five to eight, covering review techniques, rating, and feedback, coaching and counselling skills. Another approach would be to start with the introductory course (modules 1 to 4), then go through the basics of conducting discussions, rating and providing feedback and then run a later, more advanced course on coaching and counselling.

MONITORING AND EVALUATING PERFORMANCE APPRAISAL

Clearly, it is important to monitor the introduction of performance appraisal very carefully but it is equally vital to continue to monitor and evaluate it regularly, especially after its first year of operation.

The best method of monitoring and evaluation is to ask those involved – appraisers and appraisees – how it worked. As many as possible should be seen, individually and in groups, to discuss their experiences. The questions put should be open-ended along the following lines:

○ How did you feel the discussion went?

○ Did you feel that it covered the key issues?

○ Were both parties fully involved?

○ Was the discussion friendly and open?

○ Were the conclusions reached helpful and fair?

○ Were any problems met by either appraisers or appraisees during the discussion?

○ At the end of the discussion were both parties clear, and in agreement, on what they had to do?

○ Did you have any problems in completing the forms?

○ Overall, to what extent do you think this was a worthwhile exercise?

○ Are there any improvements needed to the process?

It is also desirable to scrutinise a sample of completed forms to check on how well and thoroughly they have been completed.

The evaluation can be carried out by members of the project team and/or by the human resources function. An independent consultant or adviser can be used to conduct a special review.

Individual and group discussions can be supplemented by a special survey of reactions to performance appraisal which could be completed anonymously by all managers and staff. The results should be fed back to all concerned and analysed to assess the need for any amendments to the process or further training requirements. An example of such a survey is given in Appendix E.

The ultimate test, of course, is analysing organisational performance to establish the extent to which improvements can be attributed to performance appraisal. It may be difficult to establish a direct connection but more detailed assessments with managers and staff on the impact of the process may reveal specific areas in which there have been improvements.

APPENDICES

Appendix A

Examples of Job Descriptions

PRODUCTION DIRECTOR

Principal Accountabilities

1. Plan and control all production management activities to ensure that output, quality and customer service targets and standards are achieved.
2. Maximise productivity.
3. Optimise resource utilisation.
4. Minimise manufacturing, inventory, maintenance and distribution costs.
5. Develop new technology applications to meet defined needs and introduce improved systems for planning and control purposes.
6. Ensure that healthy and safe systems of work are maintained.
7. Increase the levels of skill motivation and commitment in the workforce.
8. Maintain a cooperative climate of employee relations.

Objectives

1. Consistently meet demand forecasts by achieving the manufacturing programmes as set out in the Master Production Schedule.
2. Reduce the level of defects from 1.5 to 1.0 per cent over the next six months.

3. Increase units produced per employee by 3 per cent over the next nine months.

4. Maintain delivery to customers within five working days of receiving the works order.

5. Reduce downtime by 2 per cent over the next six months.

6. Reduce cost per unit of output by 2 per cent over the next six months.

7. Plan and introduce a fully effective system of MRPII within the next 12 months.

8. Conduct a comprehensive health and safety audit by the end of the year which generates practical recommendations on the measures required to meet company health and safety policy requirements and to achieve the company's targets for reducing accidents and work-related health problems.

9. Develop in conjunction with the human resources depart-ment a skill-based pay scheme with supporting training programmes for introduction within 18 months.

10. Settle all disputes and grievances at shop floor level without invoking the formal disputes or grievance procedure.

REGIONAL SALES MANAGER

Principal Accountabilities

1. Plan and control regional sales effort to achieve and as far as possible, exceed sales volume and contribution targets.

2. Open new accounts in the region to achieve sales develop-ment targets.

3. Achieve agreed levels of customer service with regard to delivery, handling queries and complaints, and after-sales service.

4. Take part as required in new product launches, including pilot testing.

5. Maintain close contact with customers in order generally to promote sales and specifically to obtain marketing intelligence on trends in customer wants and needs.

6. Track competitive activity in the region in order to provide information to assist in developing marketing strategies.

7. Staff the region with high quality area managers and sales representatives who are trained, developed and motivated to achieve demanding sales targets and high levels of customer service.

Objectives

1. Achieve sales and contribution targets as set out in the current three month sales budget for the region.

2. Open at least 50 potentially profitable new accounts over the next six months.

3. Ensure that:
   — in conjunction with the regional distribution depot, deliveries from stock are made within three working days;
   — immediate reports are made to headquarters of any failure to meet delivery standards arising from the goods not being made available on time to the depot by manufacturing or distribution;
   — customer orders are processed within 24 hours;
   — customer requests for after-sales service are acknowledged within 24 hours and satisfied within three working days.

4. Complete the pilot testing of new product X in conjunction with the product development department within three months.

5. Provide prompt customer and competitor intelligence which provides marketing with valuable insights as a basis for formulating marketing, product development and pricing strategies.

6. Ensure that:
   — the turnover of sales representatives is reduced from an average of 2.2 per cent per month to an average of 1.5 per cent by the end of the year;

— all newly recruited sales representatives attend the first basic sales training course available after they join;

— area sales managers implement the company's sales development programme in full for each of their sales representatives.

HUMAN RESOURCES MANAGER

Principal Accountabilities

1. Advises on human resources strategies, policies and practices in order to ensure that the company has the high quality, well-motivated and commited workforce it needs.

2. Prepare demand and supply forecasts of human resource requirements and plans for the recruitment and retention of employees to meet business requirements.

3. Provide a recruitment and selection service to meet the company's needs.

4. Provide advice on all employment and health and safety matters, including issues arising in connection with employment legislation, to ensure that the company meets its legal and social obligations and avoids legal actions.

5. Develop and help to implement effective performance management processes.

6. Plan and implement training and development programmes to meet identified needs and satisfy the company's requirements for an effective and multiskilled workforce.

7. Advise on reward management systems and the operation of the company's pay structure and performance pay schemes.

8. Advise on employee relations issues and coordinate the company's involvement and communication processes in order to develop and maintain a cooperative and peaceful climate of employee relations in the company.

9. Develop and maintain an effective computerised personnel information system.

Objectives

1. Introduce new performance management system by ...
2. Increase the ratio of suggestions to the number of employees by x per cent.
3. Revise the current equal opportunities policy by...to conform to best practice.
4. Improve the satisfaction index based on the client/user survey by y per cent.

Performance Standards

Performance will be up to standard when:

1. A proactive approach is consistently adopted in making proposals to management on the development of human resources policies and practices which will improve business performance and add value.
2. Realistic plans are made to anticipate future staff requirements which avoids skill shortages or unmanageable staff surpluses.
3. Systematic recruitment and selection procedures are maintained which provide a wholly acceptable service to line managers. An acceptable service being one that includes:
   — a prompt (within one working day) response to requests for advice or help in recruitment;
   — the delivery of acceptable job descriptions, person specifications, draft advertisements and media plans within three working days;
   — the use of psychometric tests which have been properly evaluated, are administered by trained staff and provide valuable insights for selection purposes;
   — the delivery of a short list of candidates by an agreed deadline who meet the specification, supported by helpful profiles.
4. Helpful advice is given on employment and health and safety matters which is based on a thorough understanding of the

relevant legislation and company policies and procedures. The advice is such that the company is not involved in any tribunal or other form of legal action.

5. Performance management is introduced by the end of the year, the pilot tests having shown that the approach is acceptable to managers and staff and full preliminary briefing and training programmes having taken place.

6. Training programmes are based on a systematic analysis of needs and meet success criteria as established by programme and course evaluations.

7. Reward management policies and practices are developed which ensure that rewards are both competitive and equitable and contribute to the attraction, motivation and retention of staff within cost budgets. Reward reviews are conducted efficiently (ie on time and accurately) and managers are provided with practical and helpful advice on their responsibilities for managing rewards in their departments.

8. A good climate of employee relations is maintained as indicated by the outcomes of employee attitude surveys and the absence of disputes or references to the grievance procedure.

9. The computerised personnel information system is used to maintain accurate records and to generate information for human resource planning purposes.

RETAIL MARKETING ANALYST

Main Tasks

1. Provide annual and monthly forecasts of retail sales on the basis of given assumptions to assist in generating retail one and three year plans.

2. Maintain database of information on sales, retail prices and customer discounts.

3. Provide information on products to the trade and other interested parties.

4. Deal with queries on products and prices from customers.

5. Provide general support to marketing and sales managers in analysing retail sales data.

6. Undertake special investigations and *ad hoc* exercises as required to support marketing and sales planning activities.

Performance Standards

Performance will be up to standard when:

1. Sales forecasts are properly based on given assumptions accurate and produced on time.

2. The sales statistics database is updated within one working day on receipt of weekly sales revenue returns and is maintained accurately.

3. Current information is supplied promptly (ie on the same day) to the trade and other parties.

4. Queries on products and prices from customers are answered within one working day and customers express satisfaction with the service they provide.

5. Marketing and sales managers are satisfied with the quality of the support they receive and the accuracy of the information provided.

6. Special investigations and *ad hoc* exercises are completed to satisfaction of marketing and sales managers.

WORD PROCESSOR OPERATOR

Main Tasks

1. Use word processor to produce letters, memoranda, reports and tables from handwritten drafts.

2. Assist generally with administrative activities – filing, photocopying, answering telephones etc.

3. Operate fax machine and distribute incoming messages.

4. Deputises for receptionist as required.

Performance Standards

Performance is up to standard:

1. When the operator is fully capable of using the word processor and its associated programmes to produce high quality documents.

2. An accurate, speedy and helpful service is provided to users.

3. Filing is carried out accurately and the backlog is not more than one working week.

4. Telephone callers and people met at reception are dealt with efficiently and politely.

Appendix B

Example of Performance Appraisal Form

PERFORMANCE APPRAISAL FORM

Name:	Job title
Department	Review period From: To:

Comments on achievement of objectives

Comments on achievement of competency levels

Comments on progress in meeting development/training plan

PERFORMANCE AGREEMENT

Name:	Job title
Department	Review period From: To:

Agreed performance objectives (state performance measures)

Agreed competency requirements

Agreed development/training plan

Signed	Individual	Date
	Reviewer	Date

SUMMARY

Overall level of achievement ☐	
VE = very effective E = effective D = developing B = basic	

Comments on achievements during review period

Individual's comments

Comments on any points arising from review

Reviewer's manager's comments

	Reviewer		Date
Signed	Individual		Date
	Reviewer's manager		Date

Appendix C

Checklist – Factors Affecting Managerial Performance

The performance management process contains an analysis of what has been achieved in relation to objectives and the factors which have affected performance. This provides the basis for agreeing what should be achieved in the future and deciding what needs to be done to ensure that any factors within the individual's control which have affected performance are dealt with in the next review period. This may mean developing strengths or taking steps to overcome any problems, such as gaps in knowledge or skills.

The following checklist is designed to help managers identify and discuss the factors which may have affected performance. These factors will, of course, vary considerably from job to job so that this checklist will have to be used selectively.

FACTORS WHICH MAY BE OUTSIDE OR NOT COMPLETELY WITHIN THE MANAGER'S CONTROL

1. Unforeseeable changes in the circumstances in which the job is carried out – either internal or imposed by external events.
2. Poorly defined responsibilities.
3. Inappropriate or unachievable objectives or targets.
4. Insufficient guidance or support from the manager or other individuals at higher levels in the organisation.

5. Inadequate cooperation or support from colleagues.

6. Inadequate resources – money, staff, equipment or time.

7. Insufficient training.

8. The job demands levels of skill or knowledge which the individual does not have and could not reasonably be expected to possess.

FACTORS WHICH MAY BE WITHIN THE MANAGER'S CONTROL

The following provides guidelines on the standard of performance which managers can reasonably be expected to achieve. These should be discussed and agreed, with any modifications thought appropriate, in the performance agreement meeting. The extent to which there is an inability to reach any of these standards should be discussed and agreed.

1. **Leadership**
   — Develops cohesive groups and teamwork.
   — Guides others to the accomplishment of objectives.
   — Resolves conflicts.
   — Provides direction under uncertain conditions.

2. **Managing skills**
   — Delegates work responsibility among employees for maximum efficiency.
   — Monitors employees' performance to achieve organisational goals and maintain control.
   — Sets clear, understandable objectives and priorities for department, self and with each employee.
   — Schedules and develops contingency plans.
   — Motivates people towards effective, cooperative group and individual efforts.

3. **Human resource development**

— Conducts performance reviews according to established guidelines.

— Provides good feedback to employees at the time of the event and in performance review meetings.

— Praises and recognises positive performance of employees; builds confidence in employees by supporting their appropriate decisions and actions.

— Takes prompt corrective measures when employees' performance needs improvement.

— Encourages and assists individuals through coaching, training and other methods to acquire knowledge, skills and expertise necessary for effective job performance and promotion.

4. **Decision making and problem solving**

— Identifies and anticipates potential problems.

— Recognises critical situations and takes appropriate action.

— Investigates and analyses problems and situations adequately and appropriately for the circumstances.

— Solicits and encourages ideas and input from others, involving them in the decision making process.

— Considers the whole organisation when making decisions.

— Looks for, evaluates and considers alternatives and options in solving problems prior to making decisions and recommendations.

— Willing to accept responsibility for decisions whatever the outcome.

5. **Innovation/creativity**

— Recommends new methods and ideas.

— Accepts ideas and builds on them; adds value to given efforts.

— Questions constructively why things are done in a particular way.

6. **Flexibility/adaptability**

— Willing to accept new assignments and complete them according to set standards.

— Can handle a wide variety of assignments.

— Willing to consider new ideas and methods.

— Open to constructive criticism and suggestions.

7. **Cooperativeness**

— Collaborates effectively with colleagues and other internal departments.

— Obtains cooperation from others.

8. **Responsiveness**

— Understands and responds to needs and requests quickly and willingly.

— Makes his/her expertise available to others.

— Represents the department's services in a precise and acceptable manner.

9. **Communication**

— Communicates all matters of importance up and down the organisation in an accurate, timely manner.

— Provides complete and reliable information.

— Participates easily and influentially in meetings.

— Listens carefully to others.

— Writes clearly, concisely, accurately and persuasively.

— Speaks clearly, concisely, accurately and persuasively.

10. **Technical/professional knowledge**

— Has the knowledge required in specified areas to achieve objectives.

11. **Technical/professional skill**

— Has the skills required in specified areas to achieve objectives.

IDENTIFYING CAUSES

The extent to which the reason for the individual's behaviour in not achieving the expected and agreed standards is because of inadequate ability or skill or is the result of the individual's attitude should be jointly determined and agreed.

ACTION

Performance development and improvement will only take place if action is agreed to deal with any of the factors mentioned above which have been identified as contributing to poor performance.

Factors Outside the Individual's Control

In reviewing these factors the discussion should consider the extent to which the individual might have been able to anticipate or reduce his or her impact by, for example, discussing them thoroughly with his or her manager. The steps that should be taken if these factors reoccur in the future should also be discussed.

Factors Within the Individual's Control

The actions which can be taken to deal with these factors include:

○ the individual agreeing what has to be done by himself or herself – this can be expressed as a development need in the performance agreement;

○ the manager agreeing with the individual a programme of on-the-job developmental training; this may include coaching, counselling or extended experience with appropriate training and guidance;

○ the manager agreeing and recommending specific training courses to extend knowledge or enhance skills.

Appendix D

Analysis of Performance Problems

If the target or standard of performance has not been achieved there will be a performance problem. The causes of this problem can be analysed under the following headings:

1. **The problem is caused by somebody else:**
    — unforeseeable changes in job requirements arising from external or internal pressures;
    — expected resources not available;
    — lack of co-operation;
    — interference.

2. **The problem is caused by the manager:**
    — failing to clarify requirements and expectations – objectives, standards and priorities;
    — failing to provide adequate encouragement, guidance, support or information;
    — expecting too much – setting unreasonable or unattainable objectives or standards;
    — arbitrarily changing tasks or priorities.

3. **The problem arises because of the individual's:**
    — lack of knowledge;
    — lack of skill;
    — failure to understand task or objectives;
    — lack of confidence;

— lack of application and effort;

— failure to conform to policies or procedures;

— lack of interest;

— negative or uncooperative attitude;

— failure to get priorities right;

— carelessness.

NOTES

○ These categories will probably overlap. It is most unlikely that there is any single cause of the problem. For example, the problem may be the individual's lack of ability, but this may have been compounded by new and unforeseen demands and/or a failure on the part of the manager to ensure that the individual had the necessary knowledge and skills.

○ It would be reasonable to expect the individual to make some attempt to try and overcome problems caused by other people or even his/her manager (if objectives are not understood, for example, individuals can always ask for clarification).

○ The aim of both parties should be to avoid getting into a defensive position. Respect is lost through defending mistakes, not admitting them.

WAYS OF HELPING INDIVIDUALS TO IMPROVE

Knowledge and skill problems

○ Coaching by line manager.

○ On and off-the-job training.

○ Reading lists/distance learning/computer-based learning.

○ Assignment to new tasks (job enlargement).

○ Job rotation.

Failure to understand task or objectives

○ Review of existing job description with line manager.
○ Review and clarification of objectives with line manager.
○ Discussions with fellow team members and colleagues.

Lack of confidence

○ Counselling by manager.
○ Help from fellow team members.
○ Counselling by another party (internal or external).

Failures concerning priorities or procedures

○ Improvement targets.
○ Coaching by manager.

Lack of application or effort

○ Improvement targets.

Attitude problems

○ Counselling.
○ Improvement targets.
○ New job.

Appendix E

Performance Appraisal Evaluation Form

FOR COMPLETION BY APPRAISEES

1. How effectively was your appraisal discussion conducted by your appraiser in each of the areas listed below ? Rate as follows:

   1=very effectively
   2=effectively
   3=fairly effectively
   4=not very effectively

   Rating
   — creating and maintaining an informal and friendly atmosphere;
   — working to a clear structure;
   — using praise;
   — handling criticism;
   — giving you ample opportunity to express your point of view;
   — listening to what you had to say;
   — focusing on facts.

3. Were objectives agreed during the meeting? Yes/no.
4. If yes, are they reasonable? Yes/no.
5. Was a plan of action agreed at the end of the meeting? Yes/no.

6. If so, do you think it was reasonable? Yes/no.
7. How would you rate the overall effectiveness of the meeting:
   — very effective;
   — effective;
   — fairly effective;
   — ineffective?
8. How did you feel after the meeting:
   — highly motivated;
   — reasonably well motivated;
   — not very well motivated;
   — demotivated?
9. Comments – reasons for the ratings given above:

Appendix F

Examples of performance appraisal and performance management schemes

CAMBRIDGESHIRE COUNTY COUNCIL

The main features of the Cambridgeshire County Council approach are as follows:

○ define the purpose of the job and the results to be attained. These accountabilities are directly linked to the job-holder's role in achieving the organisation's objectives. For lower-graded staff, accountabilities have been replaced with a more flexible and simple system of tasks and duties that is felt to be more appropriate and measurable for assessing performance.

○ **Performance measures** relating to money, time, effect and reaction are used to assess the achievement of accountabilities.

○ **Performance standards** are used to set acceptable levels of performance.

○ **Goals** are used to help staff concentrate on special results which need to be achieved from within their accountabilities.

○ **Action plans** are prepared to assist staff in meeting their accountabilities or goals.

○ **Progress reviews** Annual reviews are held to assess what has been accomplished in the previous year, to agree what is to be achieved in the following year, to help staff improve performance, and to clarify the job-holder's career prospects, aspirations and intentions. Following the review the job-holder is given a rating which has to be accepted by both sides as fair.

Each of the job-holder's accountabilities is also rated on a five point scale. A confirming appraiser has a dual role as a quality controller of performance standards and as an arbiter to act between the job-holder and manager in any disagreement.

○ **Performance-related pay** Some job-holders, if budget limits allow, are awarded a non-consolidated cash payment following a high performance rating.

ICL

ICL follows an integrated approach to performance management by linking a number of different processes within a performance management framework. Individual objectives are set which support the achievement of business strategies. Formal assessment of performance against these objectives leads to personal job improvement and training plans and a performance rating which influences the pay review. The output of these processes leads to periodic organisational management reviews which are concerned with developing the organisational capability of ICL. These directly impact on business strategies.

NATIONAL AUSTRALIA GROUP

Following discussions with staff, the following suggestions were made on why performance management was needed:

○ We need to be offered encouragement and support to perform well.

○ When our performance is assessed it needs to be as objective as possible.

○ We should all be part of the same process of performance assessment.

○ We need to believe and have confidence in a system which is fair to everyone.

○ We need everybody to be trained so that the approach is fully understood and can be applied consistently.

O We all need to be involved in the process with advance information, time for preparation and an opportunity to assess ourselves.

Performance management works in stages that represent a cycle from the initial planning of the individual's performance and development to the final appraisal at the end of the period.

The starting-points for measuring performance are the operational requirements. These are described as certain tasks which have to be carried out by individuals to do their jobs successfully.

Objectives are defined as specific activities/tasks to be undertaken and completed during an agreed period of time. Each objective must have a prescribed measurable outcome indicating the required level of performance. This enables subsequent measurement to be more effective.

In setting objectives staff are asked to focus on key areas of their job and consider how they will contribute to the key value drivers (KVDs) of the business which are:

O customer relationships;

O human resource management;

O growth/volumes;

O earnings;

O productivity;

O risk management;

O capitalisation.

To measure the achievement of objectives staff are asked to state the performance outcomes expected. These outcomes are called key result areas (KRAs).

Performance criteria are expressed as aspects of performance which include both attributes and competences. These are the knowledge, skills and experiences needed to complete work successfully (attributes) and the particular abilities staff are able to display (competences).

In the second stage of the performance planning process staff are asked to look at the way in which they can improve the knowledge, skills, attitudes and behaviour affecting their performance. This is done by reference to ten performance criteria (these were listed in Chapter 8).

To help staff to agree with their manager what is expected of them a set of performance guidelines was produced which describe each performance criteria in detail (see Chapter 8). Staff are asked to refer to guidelines to provide broad definitions of what is expected of them at the appropriate job level. The definitions are regarded only as indicators and staff can use definitions from adjacent columns as appropriate for their particular job. These planned standards are then used at the appraisal stage as part of the performance evaluation.

The performance appraisal is conducted jointly by the individual and the appraiser to assess how well the individual has achieved his/her performance plan. The result is recorded in a Performance Planning and Appraisal Form.

The performance development plan provides for a review of the previous development plan and the description of a new development plan which provides answers to three questions posed by the appraiser:

○ Which areas of your performance do you feel are in need of development?

○ What can I do to help to improve your performance?

○ What activities do you plan to improve your performance?

Further space is provided for suggestions in training requirements, the individual's progress in developing knowledge and skills and career preferences.

NHS WALES

The overall objectives of performance management are defined as being to 'reflect and reinforce the strategic intent of the NHS on Wales and our continuing commitment to the "PEOPLE" principles'. Its focus therefore includes:

○ Contribution of commissioners and providers to health gain.

○ Reaffirmation of the need to value people as individuals.

○ Achievement of the most cost-effective balance in the use of resources at every level and locality within NHS Wales.

The focus for performance improvement in different jobs are described as changing between three types:

○ **Output targets** – 'hard' measurable output targets often derived from accountability statements, eg within job or role descriptions.

○ **Competences** – the display of certain professional skills and behavioural competences (eg listening, organisation of others, managing people) which are the 'how' beyond the output achieved.

○ **Tasks** – the completion of certain predetermined tasks to the required standards.

POWERGEN

The performance discussion usually takes place between April and June each year. The assessor is expected to prepare for the meeting by collecting the relevant facts and contacting the relevant managers for their views of the assessee's performance. The performance assessment meeting focuses on both past performance and future objectives. Following the meeting, the assessor completes the relevant documentation and this is passed on to the assessee for comment. Subsequently, the assessor's manager reviews both the assessment and the employee's comments to check for consistency and fairness and to ensure that the individual's objectives will meet business needs. Interim meetings are expected to take place throughout the year to monitor performance against objectives. At the end of the review period the assessor arranges the next annual assessment meeting.

ROYAL SOCIETY FOR MENTALLY HANDICAPPED CHILDREN AND ADULTS (MENCAP)

In contrast, the performance and development management scheme introduced recently by MENCAP emphasises, as its title implies, both the performance improvement and developmental aspects of the process. It too is based on individual objectives related to the Society's mission and strategic plans, but these lead exclusively to performance improvement and development plans; there is no performance rating or performance related pay.

STANDARD CHARTERED BANK

At Standard Chartered performance is assessed by reference to individual capability against job competences, and to individual achievement against personal objectives. Competences are defined as the skills staff need to develop if they are to perform to a fully satisfactory standard in their work. They can be weighted according to the demands of particular jobs. Both competences and objectives must be set in line with the company's business strategies and aims. Staff who are rated as having exceeded requirements normally receive a performance payment. Those who 'meet' the requirement do not necessarily receive a payment and there is a further selection process within this category.

ZENECA PHARMACEUTICALS

The purpose of performance management at Zeneca Pharmaceuticals is to 'improve business performance by raising each individual's effectiveness'. The process was designed to answer business needs and was focused on developing people rather than assessment.

The process is intended to produce the following benefits:

○ clearer business objectives and personal targets, with an improved correlation between the two;

○ an emphasis on developing individuals to help them achieve their targets;

○ a closer relationship between individuals, involving coaching, encouragement and motivation;

○ a more objective assessment of performance against targets, leading to a more performance-related reward system.

The key features of the performance management system are:

○ Individuals are aligned with the business, are clear about their roles, where they fit in and what they contribute. Clarifying strategic business objectives from which functional and departmental objectives and individual objectives follow was crucial to this task. Its success depended on it not being just a top-down, one way flow, but an iterative one involving a realistic degree of shared discussion and feedback.

○ Evaluated job descriptions, written in a standard format containing job purpose and principal accountabilities, enabled a crucial shift in emphasis reinforcing a business-led approach and the focus on contribution, not tasks. Significantly, the job descriptions of line managers include their people management responsibilities.

○ Individual targets are agreed within business, unit or team objectives and job accountabilities and are critical to performance in the job. Development plans are based on these targets primarily but may cover anticipated future needs.

Index